WHEN HE
Walks Away

Hearing God When Your
Husband Leaves Your Marriage

MARY A. BRYANT

ISBN 978-1-64349-884-3 (paperback)
ISBN 978-1-64349-885-0 (digital)

Christian Faith Publishing, Inc.
832 Park Avenue
Meadville, PA 16335
www.christianfaithpublishing.com

Printed in the United States of America

To Emma, Meredith, Cole, and Hope,
You are my heart.

For all of us who seek an anchor in the storm.

*Fear not, for I have redeemed you; I have
summoned you by name; you are mine.*
—Isaiah 43:1

INTRODUCTION

The Great Divide

I WOULD LIKE TO SAY that I am writing this from the other side. I am, mostly; but there are still places that seep out, bleeding from the trauma of it all. It catches me more often than I would like to admit, but I am getting better. We all somehow get better.

I heard it said that one teaches what it is they want most to learn for themselves. If this is true, and I believe it is, then I am qualified to share this journey with you. I've got the stripes of one who's been through the war of broken hearts. I've earned this rank, not because I wanted to, but because I *had* to. But then again, if you are reading this, you have also. We are compadres.

I am cautioned here because I know that in the scope of life, in all the unspeakable things that people survive—the desperation of watching a loved one die, the incomprehensible pain that comes with tragedy and great loss—abandonment seems like a fair trade. I mean to never make what I have gone through, what you are going through, more devastating than what others have survived. It doesn't take much to imagine worse scenarios. We hear about them every day.

But this so feels like death, doesn't it? One day, you think your world is relatively stable. You're married or in relationship with someone you've built your world around; and then in one reprehensible moment, they pull up stakes and walk away. You are left gasping for breath, unable to conceive the thought that life could possibly go on. Your world, and everything in it, comes crashing down in heaps and piles of brokenness. You are suddenly Humpty Dumpty. I know. I've been on that wall too.

However, I am here to tell you the truth: you will survive this. More than this, you will thrive again. Though I understand how these words may ring hollow to your shattered spirit, you can *and will* come out of this better than before the war began, and I'll prove it.

First, let me say that this battle you are in is so much less about you than it is about the man that left. If you are the one who stayed, fighting for your relationship, putting all you had into saving it, I acknowledge you. I know how it feels to have devastation handed to you on a not-so-silver platter. I commend you for standing in this pain and for your efforts to find reason with what is not, for you, an acceptable alternative to staying together. Though your husband has likely given you his thin and "justifiable" reasons for what he has done, you recognize that there truly is not an excuse good enough for bailing ship on your marriage when the waters get a little choppy. That is not what unconditional love does. That is just not how God intended it to work.

In my case, after nearly thirty years, my husband and father of our four young-adult children decided that life would be more fun without us. It's the classic story of midlife crisis complete with the fancy new car, new clothes, and dating websites. Your circumstances are perhaps very different than mine, but the result is the same. Half of you is off "finding" himself, and the other half—*you*—has been brought to a place of complete and utter collapse, and it hurts like hell.

Where do we begin? How do we know which of the broken pieces we pick up first? How do we reassemble what may be a near lifetime of dreams now shattered? How do we fill this gaping wound-edness that follows us like a shadow and won't let us rest?

There are the tangible items too that are attached to our lives such as homes, finances, pets, and Christmas decorations. Add children to the mix and there is a holy war that takes its toll on generations that has nothing at all to do with custody and visitation. The damage done is not on the surface, nor is it measured in conflicts of schedules and financial accountability. It goes much deeper than that and much greater than one can possibly know. It's catastrophic.

For you, there are waves of emotion and bouts of crying to a degree you never thought possible. Or maybe you are stoic, still too in shock to cry. There resides an empty, hollow pit within your solar plexus. That is the place your heart used to be. Every time you see a picture from the past or watch a Hallmark commercial, or an old friend sees you in the grocery store, you discover a new truth. Your heart is not done breaking, and your eyes won't stop leaking. Still.

Much needs to happen in terms of healing and though I will offer you some sound and thoughtful advice, this is not so much an attempt to tell you step-by-step how to navigate these new and choppy waters. It is to share with you and offer what I have learned on this journey.

What follows is what I believe God gave to me during my season in the pit of desperation. It is from this that I offer, as perspective, what I learned from Him while moving from survival to thriving again. It is, for me, the lessons of God's grace and mercy that made all the difference. It is what I believe that He wants for us all.

This book is salve for your woundedness. It's as much spiritual as it is practical. It's a compilation of what it takes to righteously get through the layers of emotional pain—the mourning, the angst. It's a way of saying, "Me too. That's what it feels like for me too."

I want you to know that I share this journey with you and in sharing my story, I hope you will find courage, strength, and hope for your own.

I want you to know, it will get better.

I want you to know as well, importantly, that this is not a linear process. It's a jagged one. It's one of two steps forward, three steps back, and many variations of that. It's a process of constantly reorienting where you are and where you're going. Soon you will find yourself learning to navigate the waters with deft awareness, no longer prone to be so easily tossed about in them. Like every other day, you'll have moments of calm and then find that the least bit aggravation will put you in a tailspin. It's all part of the journey. It's normal.

In the end, you will arrive at a place of understanding. Everything you are going through will not suddenly make perfect sense, but in time, you will gain a fresh perspective. It will cause you to become grounded, to understand what really matters. You will realize what is truly worth fighting for and what you can simply chalk up to lessons learned. You may still miss your husband, or you may find his absence is making room for your new season, your new life, and be able to find hope in that.

It is my prayer that these pages hold for you a platform from which to stand and look out over the expanse of what has happened and reassess what it all means. I pray that you will come to understand that all things truly do work out for the good when we trust God to tend to all that is broken.

I know of people who find that things come full circle. Their husbands come to their senses and want another chance at making their marriage work. Partners realize that the grass really isn't greener somewhere else. Spouses recall what brought them together in the first place, and reconnect and recommit. Even my own parents, after nearly twenty years divorced and other marriages in between, got back together and remarried, staying together until the end.

There are plenty of statistics too that uphold the opposite. Men who never return, who never look back, and who compartmentalize their existence in a woman's life to the point of cruel narcissistic denial. They simply close the door and move on.

My hope is that after grieving, you will be like many women who find in the mirror a person they come to realize has long been forgotten. Even in the best of circumstances, life can often distort our self-image, our potential, and our capacity to believe again in the impossible. We compromise, acquiesce, and live our lives in half-measures to get along and play nice.

What if God wants more for us? What if God wants us to be fulfilled in Him first, so that we can bring a new vitality and spirit to all our relationships? In God, we are restored and renewed in ways that can truly be miraculous. Transforming our lives, even when such transitions are forced upon us, can bring blessings and fulfillment.

It's okay if you don't believe it yet. It will come.

This is not about false hope. The void left behind by your former half is real and gaping. This is the story of wholeness—*your* wholeness, the rebuilding of your life. It's about discovering what is beyond this intensity of transition and finding a happier place within yourself.

Whether your husband never returns, or in time, God convicts his heart to repent and reconcile, you are not alone. My hope is that regardless of the ultimate outcome, you will find peace and the return of joy.

It can happen, and it will.

I remember
When love was young
And so was I
And so was he, this man who is now a stranger to me
Despite four kids
Twenty-eight Christmases
And countless conversations
On pillows and across table tops
He is now off-limits, empty
And I am alone
Though my kids surround me, still
It is a broken me—
A fractured half of what once was whole
Forgive me, Lord
When fear overtakes my Spirit
Help me, Father, when I spiral into the abyss of despair
I will live again
I will be whole again
I will know peace and love and understanding again
I will
I will
Because You love me

From the author's journal

1

Red Sky in Morning, Sailors Take Warning

IF YOU ARE LIKE me, then you have found yourself shipwrecked, in a bazillion pieces strewn across some foreign land that looks like home but feels desperately unlike any place you've ever been. It's not fun, this place. It hurts like hell. You might find yourself simply walking among the artifacts of what was once your life, searching for clues, for signs of where it all went wrong. You circle and pace, and circle again, and nothing adds up. Nothing makes sense.

Even in the most difficult circumstances, you still can't believe that your husband, your partner, would just leave. As though he simply stood up one day, brushed the dirt off his trousers and said, "See ya." You never expected the finality of it. This is someone you love. This is someone you shared your dreams with, speaking pillow to pillow about all that your heart ever longed for. You may well have had your babies with this man. You have a lifetime of trust, a covenant, and a treasure trove of memories that are wonderful.

Then *poof*, he is gone.

I told a friend, months after my husband left, that it felt to me like I was a prop for that old magic trick where the magician saws a woman in half and then waves his wand, spins the table, and suddenly, she appears whole again. Only for me, the trick ended badly. The sawing part happened for sure, but somehow, I was still half a woman—one leg, one arm, and part of a torso. It felt as though I was still bleeding on the table. The magician had left the building. No one remained in the audience. Half of what was me was abruptly amputated.

The friend I shared this with was like many who felt empathy for the intense emotional upheaval of my situation. There were others who could somewhat relate, recalling past break ups that had not gone well. Yet it's hard to convey it all, isn't it? It's hard to believe that anyone could truly know the devastation of what was once your seemingly normal, happy life. You want so desperately to understand how you wound up in this gut-wrenching place. Alone. Unable to discern any resemblance to the life you knew. It's impossible to share an emptiness that cannot be defined with words.

Of course, I do not know your every circumstance, but I can tell you with all certainty that you likely pondered endlessly every argument, every off-the-cuff remark your husband made. Every time you found him disengaged or uninterested in what you shared, felt, or cared about came flooding back to you. You might even blame yourself thinking, as many of us do, that somehow you are not enough. It must be that you are unlovable or unworthy of your husband's affection.

This, I assure you, is a lie. What has happened is less about *you* and more about him. *He* is the one who walked away, broke covenant, unfaithful in some discrete or blatant way. If it wasn't another woman, then it was with himself, in what he allowed to separate his devotion, his promise to love you until his last breath. Indeed, it's about his very honor.

Perhaps there was nothing at all that flagged your husband's departure. For all you knew, everything was fine. Perhaps one day, he just decided to throw in the towel in a vague search for happiness that he is convinced exists outside your marriage and domain. Somewhere in the transaction, however, the conclusion is drawn that you simply could not supply what he needed anymore. Another lie.

Every marriage has conflicts and issues. Every marriage. Not just yours and mine. Storms and seasons, and difficulties come and go. Together, you are to work things out, to endure and persevere. But when one stops seeking resolutions or becomes disengaged, then the function of the union deteriorates. Whether it happens suddenly or in a slow crawl that takes your marriage over a cliff of complacency, it cannot survive without help. The desire to mend it requires both parties present and participating. It takes two to tango. It's not sufficient to merely tap our toe to the music. We must be, if not completely instep with our partner, at least holding on or being led. It simply doesn't work otherwise.

When one person in the marriage withdraws his dance card and leaves, all that is left besides countless unanswered questions is what we see and feel about ourselves. Our minds tell us we are no longer the prettiest girl at the ball. As if one day, our husband figured out that our glass slippers are really sneakers, and our gowns are made of denim and tee shirts. What a disappointment we must be! Whatever perceived insufficiencies he left you with, Prince Charming got on his horse and rode off into the sunset, and you are left banished from his kingdom and life as you knew it.

This is exactly what Satan, the enemy, would have you think. *If only* you had been more loving, kind, understanding. *If only* you had told your husband more often how much you appreciated him, needed him, wanted him, *then* he would be with you now instead of at the bar, at his friend's house, or in Timbuktu.

"If onlys" have one purpose—to discourage you even more. The more beaten down you become, the more willing you are to accept blame, to second-guess everything about yourself and your life. It's a tactic that is so insidious, so effective, we don't even realize it is happening. Satan is a clever foe.

I've had a dance or two with the enemy. I too came to believe so many lies about myself. I was convinced that I was suddenly unlovable, unworthy, inadequate in every way. The seeds of these thoughts were planted during arguments and innuendoes. And what I didn't hear in his words, I deducted from my husband's behavior and in the ways he discounted me. After a while, I got pretty good at helping him, filling in the blanks myself: *I'm not a good cook, I yell at the kids, I expect too much, it's my fault the bills come in faster than the money.* The list was never ending.

It's funny how we assume so many untruths and blame while our men sit on couches, are out with the guys, and have sudden bouts of amnesia when it comes to knowing that the trash barrels go out on the same day each week for twenty years. This is not to say that, as wives, we don't have our own quirky brand of things that drive our men batty. We all have them. Yet we are quick to forget a very fundamental truth—marriage is a partnership. Whatever is good, or whatever is not, requires contributions by both parties.

The Bible tells us what God thinks about love.

> *Love is patient, love is kind. It does not envy, it does not boast, it is not proud. It is not rude, it is not self-seeking, it is not easily angered, it keeps no record of wrongs. Love does not delight in evil but rejoices with the truth. It always protects, always trusts, always hopes, always perseveres. (1 Cor. 13:4–7)*

So where does it say that there are conditions? Footnotes? Exclusions? Clauses that are non-binding? Is there a statute of limitations? Nowhere does it give exceptions to the design God spoke for it. And just so that we don't misinterpret His commands, it sums it all up with these three words: "Love never fails."

But sometimes, it seems it does.

No matter how much we do our part, loving unconditionally, being who it is we feel God has called us to be as wives, there are times when it goes wrong. Does it mean that it's the end? What about a marriage where there is abuse? There are no illusions of sanctimony. Sometimes the infractions are so egregious, not only is ending such a union acceptable but most often necessary.

God intends for us to be loved, honored, and respected. Just as He intends the same for our husbands. Love is dynamic. It's a verb. It's not always perfect. It's not always wine and roses. It's staying and fighting for what is right. It's sickness and health. It's richer or poorer. God blesses marriage when both hearts are united in His righteousness.

I know you believed in your marriage. You and your husband were bound together in faith and love. You likely went to church together and raised your kids with the same prayerful convictions that held and protected you; never thinking it possible that one day, one of you would leave. Yet here you are on your own.

The enemy will undermine whatever God brought together. He's been doing it since the beginning of time. He's good at it. It's his job. Once he has a foothold, he will not stop until his work is done. The way he accomplishes his destruction in our lives comes by way of various clever schemes. He messes with our reality through our thoughts and in how we perceive our circumstances. He whispers to us about how bored and unexciting our lives are, and how uninteresting our spouses have become. He shows us ways to compare our lives, our marriages, against others and then highlights for us all the discrepancies. Once he's got us, he reels us in by tempting us. The world offers up a host of seductive illusions to whet one's whistle while Satan slips in the poison.

If that is not enough, now that the evil one has messed with your husband, he's coming for *you*. Satan wants to keep you discouraged, weary, and isolated because that is when he can do his best work. He is not satisfied to just kill your relationship with your man. He also will bring you down to the lowest point possible so you will give up, or give in, to anything that he suggests.

The thief comes only to steal and kill and destroy. (John 10:10)

The antidote to a lie is truth. Sometimes it takes being broken for the light of truth to come to us through the cracks. I beg you to hear me: *you must stop believing the lies that say you are not enough.* You must stop thinking that you aren't worthy of love and that is why your husband left. You must stop making the responsibility for keeping your marriage intact as being solely yours. The ploy to get you to bear all blame is typical and effective. It works well, but it is built on complete deception.

Your husband is not the first one to be lured away. This is not to call him innocent. It's not to excuse him on any level. He became a willing participant of the scheme, armed with bite-sized justifications such as "needing a change" and just wanting "to be happy." And that, on the surface, sounds almost reasonable. Coating the disillusionment with ambiguity only cloaks the fact that he no longer wants to be held accountable, nor thinks he should be. There is too much fun to be had in the mirage of sin.

We expose ourselves to the enemy's ploy by not seeking God in the solution for our struggles. When we seek the world for answers, the world will tell us what we want to hear. The louder it screams the better. The thoughts and images flash in our heads, convincing us, as if for the first time, we are seeing things as they *really* are—how very unhappy we have been, how much we are missing out on life. Then the accusations and blame come ever easier. Justifications roll off our tongues. Chaos abounds, and it doesn't care who it hurts. We are all susceptible to this hideous prank. Wives, as well as husbands, are guilty of this sin.

Now one of you has left.

For our husbands, thoughts such as these became entrenched, taking on a life of their own. As though finding himself in a maze, from every angle he looked at his life, it all looked the same. He felt trapped, unable to see that the path just before him would take him—and you—into a clearing where your marriage could breathe again. Rather than seeking help, he bolted in a rush of adrenaline that closed off all other possibilities to find your way out together and intact. He has, I'm sure, concocted his case and defense of any argument you may have given him to consider. He is planted in the fantasy of a new life and has thrown all his marbles into the game. Hook, line, and sinker, he has taken the bait.

To support what has now happened, there are justifications that come with names such as midlife crisis, depression, and a nonspecific generalization of just wanting to be "happy." As real as some of these conditions are, they take a swath of our life with them in their wake. They create a scorched-earth mentality that knows no variance of cordiality. They are bent on destruction. They brand as "victims" those who are labeled by them. As if they should be excused for their behavior, victims are rendered incapable of leaving gently or with respect of relationship. Although it happens with women too, in our case, it is our men who rip themselves from the fabric of life and seemingly have no conscience doing so. They are mere subjects in whatever epidemic has claimed them.

As if he has taken over your husband through mind control, Satan plays a non-stop reel of fun and the illusion of good times that he seems unable to resist. Suddenly, your guy is the life of his own party, and you are not invited. He is on a one-track train to a carnival in the middle of nowhere. Marriage and responsibilities are obstacles that he sheds so that he can travel unencumbered.

What he doesn't understand, however, is that the baggage he carries is his own. *You* are not what is being rejected. You represent a version of himself that he wants to escape. It's the "old" him he rejects. Your husband thinks that by leaving you, he can cut ties with himself. Another twist in Satan's plot.

It's important to keep in mind that he did not just leave you, your home, and family. He also left God's plan for his life. As appealing as it may seem to him now, this newfound freedom leads, not only to a total breakdown of relationship, but also to sin. This is God's business. Nothing goes unnoticed by God. Nothing. Before one knows it, he is long down that road that leads to regret.

Things happen on this road that are not pretty. They burden our imagination, waking us up in the middle of the night to torment.

This is that barren place where we wonder what he's doing, where he is, and who he is with. It's where insult is added to injury. Everything we have within us is taxed to the limit.

We must keep our wits, and steady our resolve. We need to ask God to infuse us with supernatural strength and endurance. We want to neither overreact in fits of nervous energy or crawl into the fetal position and give up on life. This is by far the place of our greatest desperation. It's like walking on hot coals and knowing there is nothing that will take away our pain. We have to keep walking. We have to get to the other side of this barren, difficult place.

There is nothing reasonable about abandoning a lifetime commitment. There is nothing casual about breaking a covenant. Leaving the path of righteousness at whim, or even after years of contemplation, has far-reaching consequences. Believing otherwise is perhaps the greatest lie of all.

So what do we do? How can we turn this around? How can we convince our husbands that they are making a grave, destructive error of judgement? How can we show them that the damage they are causing is not just hurting us but possibly ruining his life *and* his eternity?

The answer is both simple and excruciatingly maddening—we can't. There is nothing we can do. And there is also so much we *must* do.

Even when it seems that God has forgotten about all your cares and your marriage, stay in faith and remembrance that we serve a loving and merciful God. He knows and is concerned for all you are going through.

Sometimes, He lets us wander in the wasteland of free will. He lets us have a crack at thinking our way through problems that can only be solved by submitting to Him. He lets us dwell at the bottom of the pit so that we can know that the only way out is to look up. He's waiting for us to ask Him into our problems, hurts, and circumstances. He wants us to release the outcome to Him. Completely.

As if we are thrashing about in the ocean, the waves and fear overtake us. We must allow Him to buoy us, rescuing us from our own actions that will cause us to go under. We must stop fighting it and submit ourselves to what only we can do and let Him do the rest.

This is not to say that God caused or wanted your husband to leave you. Never. But He is in this storm with you. He is your life preserver. He will not just leave you flailing about without hope or a way to get you back to shore. He won't.

For the first several weeks after my husband left, I would wake often to the sound of my own voice whimpering in the dark. I was so burdened that rest was elusive. Over and over, I spoke out loud the same words, "Help me, Lord. Help me." There was no relief for my wounded spirit. There was no pill to take away the agony. Just breathing was an effort.

One fitful night, I felt Him respond to me with as simple a phrase as was my prayer. It calmed me. It reassured me. It restored my heart to a normal beat. "I know. Be still. I know..." It was not like a voice, but like an impression in my mind, heart, and spirit. I knew it was not my own thought. It stood out in textured context to my suffering. It drew me to Him.

My angst was so great, and His presence so overwhelming.

I sat up, clasping my hands together, and thanked Him for the peace that washed over me. God knew all that was happening. He was in control. All I could do was all *I* could do. The rest was in His hands.

It was then that I released my husband to God. It was then that my prayers took on another, deeper level. I knew that there was absolutely nothing I could do. It had to be Him. It was His fight, not mine.

Each time my anxiety flared, I would take the image of my husband in my spirit and imagine laying him at the Lord's feet. Countless times throughout the day, when fear would rise in me, I did this. There, he was safe. There, he would encounter the conviction, grace, and protection that only God could impart.

The impact was profound. This is not to say that I did not still experience hurt, frustration, and all the worry that comes with "what comes next." But it helped to release me from thinking that, of my own power, I could change what was happening. Only God could deal with my husband's conscience. Only God could convict him, changing his heart from stone back into flesh. If it was God's will, then only He could accomplish it. He is very good at finding lost sheep, even those who profess to not wanting to be found.

For the first time, I had clarity that gave me something to stand on. It freed me up to take care of my daily tasks, my kids, my work, and the preservation of my faith. God was in charge. All I needed to do was to keep giving my husband back to Him.

God wants us to seek Him in all that concerns us. This is true for our small, daily things, as it is for our marriages. Even when everything is collapsing around us—and especially then—we must seek Him. We must lay our burdens at His feet and do what only we can control. He alone is mighty in power. When we rest in knowing that God knows what He is doing, anxiety subsides. Faith is the catalyst that ignites our gaining the perspective we need especially when we are in survival mode, and nothing seems as it should be.

It is trusting Him enough to know that He works all things—*all things*—out for our good. Even as you lie in the ruins of devastation, He is working. God triumphs over Satan. Always. No matter how bad it is.

You cannot protect or insure your husband's path back to righteousness. You can only maintain your own. You cannot cause him to examine his priorities, his decisions, or to acknowledge the deep wounding that his actions have caused. All you can do is stand in what *you* know.

No matter what your husband has done, or how broken this place is that you are in right now, do not receive the lies of the enemy. Recognize them for what they are—a means to get you off track and to react. Do not allow them to infect your spirit and drag you down into hopelessness. When we are desperate, Satan succeeds in creating distractions so that we will take our eyes off God.

Be vigilant and stand in the truth of knowing you are not alone. You are worthy of love and devotion. Regardless of what has been spoken over you or what reasons were given for why your husband left, do not accept blame or self-persecution. This only furthers the deception and keeps you from healing.

Although it may be impossible right now to see an outcome outside of this terrible isolation, God is at work. Lay your husband at His feet. Be still in knowing that God knows what you are going through. He knows everything your husband has done, where he is, and what he is doing. Nothing is a surprise to Him.

Be still. He knows what to do.

> *Finally, be strong in the Lord and in His mighty power. Put on the full armor of God so that you can take your stand against the devil's schemes. For our struggle is not against flesh and blood, but against the rulers, against the authorities, against the powers of this dark world and against the spiritual forces of evil in the heavenly realms. (Eph. 6:12)*

> *Be still before the Lord and wait patiently for him. (Ps. 37:7)*

2

Be the Tree

S OME YEARS AGO, MY kids gave me a frame with a collage of pictures of them inside it. It was inscribed with the saying, "Faith is not knowing that God can. It's knowing that He will." I love this frame and what it represents so much. Especially as I look at how much they have grown and who they have become as young adults. They are healthy, strong in character and integrity, and they have the seedlings of faith that will continue to flourish and be tested as they go through their lives.

Since the moment I learned they were each within my womb, I trusted the Lord with forming them for His purpose. They are not good or righteous because of me or their dad, but because the Lord has them. He loves them. Even in the times when they turn away or struggle or fall into sin. He will make a way for them, as He will for us all.

Often, I find that I gaze at this picture frame, focusing in, long and hard, as if doing so will somehow transport me back to the time and the place of when their precious smiles where captured. It seems, in many ways, like a lifetime ago.

It's hard for me, even now as I write this, to not feel the closing of my throat, fighting back the urge to cry. How sure life was then, how steady. How happy our home was, filled to the brim with my tribe of pajama-bottomed kids. At night, after baths, there were games my husband played with them that was his own special brand of fun. We sang Barney songs and "The Song That Never Ends." They would come to find me, their arms filled with books or their favorite VHS tapes, to which more dancing, marching, and singing would occur. Life was *full*. It was every cliché you can imagine—*the best times ever*. Love spilled over in exuberance, unable to be contained. We laughed, played, prayed, and believed the best of each other. It was our "love you forever" time.

In a million years, there was never even the remotest thought that these moments, these feelings, would ever end. The kids grew, of course; but the foundation of what kept us together, what made us a family, was uncompromised. To the best of my recollection, life was perfect.

Truth be told, around the time my kids gave me this gift, the emergence of a slight crack or two had begun. As they grew older, my husband and I, of course, did too. And as each new year rang in, so too were new challenges that come with every thriving family. Elementary and middle school behind them, our kids were getting part-time jobs, cars, and taking the SATs. The economy waxed and waned, and so did our finances. And so did our patience. And so did all those things that were thought to never be conditional.

A tiny crack here, an argument there, money issues that never fully eased. Frustrated, hurtful comments made and never apologized for, and life didn't seem quite so perfect anymore. It was *good*, but the wear and tear were taking a toll. Like the string pulled on a knit sweater, we were unraveling. Hoped-for resolutions began to feel distant, foreign. "Let's just get through it until we can get together and work it out," we would tell ourselves. "Never mind that our feelings are hurt. Suck it up, buttercup! There's work to do!"

As Proverbs warns, "Hope deferred makes the heart grow sick." We had so much hope for our future at one time, but disappointment after disappointment, without relent, caused hope to fade away.

The hardest part about writing this, as it is for you thinking on your own circumstance, is that you know the scenes like a rerun that you have watched many times. You know the plot. You know the twists where somebody gets hurt. You want to yell at the screen and warn the characters not to fall in the trap.

"Don't say that to him. He's just tired from working extra hours."

"Don't blame her for the mortgage payment being late. Remember your daughter was in the emergency room that day?"

At the time, however, you put so much stock into making sure everything that needs attention is getting done that you let things slip. You think that if you can just make it until your youngest is out of diapers—or out of college—surely, you will be able to mend the broken fence your withering relationship has become.

The problem is that once you get "there," whatever goal post you have named, life has ushered in a whole other host of issues. In your mind's eye, instead of mending, you hyperfocus on the difficulties and the inadequacies, the "why things are not fair and how they would be *if only.*" That is when the blaming starts.

There is a line in *It's a Wonderful Life* when an old neighbor on his porch watches George Bailey serenade the young Mary Hatch on the sidewalk as they are coming home from the prom. The man yells out to George, "Why don't you just kiss her instead of talking her to death?"

George feigns to consider such a proposal, bemused and milking the moment. "You want me to kiss her, huh?" He carries on, extoling the possibilities of different scenarios. It's a magical depiction that makes you feel the thrill of young love every bit as if you were the real Mary Hatch.

Exasperated, the old man gives up and says, "Ah, youth is wasted on the wrong people!"

How often I have thought of this. I adore this movie! There are so many redeeming and epic reflections of life. Its celebrations amid the backdrop of sacrifice, and what it's like to stay on the road

God puts you on. Its parallel theme, I believe, is the danger we all face when life becomes too much, and we let it take away our joy. In this place, we stop believing that the magic, not only no longer exists, but has us question if it was even there in the first place. This happens when we put off or postpone the very things we need to do to protect it. We stop being proactive. We start taking each other for granted.

In the movie portrayal, you almost sense that the old man could leap off the porch, grab the shoulders of the young George as if to tell him, "Don't miss this, man! Fall in love! This is the essence of life itself!"

Instead, in his resigned and frustrated response, he seems to be rendered to the notion of his own life where perhaps the bloom has fallen off the rose, and reality is a cold substitute. The magic is gone.

So seems to be the quandary we all face at one time or another. We question the quality and sustainability of our love, our marriages. When the chemistry of youth dies down, the ordinary of everyday life consumes us, and we seemed forced to qualify what was once immeasurable and unconditional. We dare even to question if what remains is still love at all.

The answer is, of course, yes!

In Proverbs 5:18–19 Solomon speaks to this:

> *May your fountain be blessed, and may you rejoice in the wife of your youth. A loving doe, a graceful deer—may her breasts satisfy you always, may you ever be captivated by her love.*

By the words of his prayer, he suggests the vulnerability that comes when we stop recognizing the blessings that extend into our older age. That we must be careful. Even Solomon seemed to know the pitfalls of what we might call "midlife crisis" or the danger that comes from thinking that perhaps what has waned, or gone through a bit of a difficult season, is no longer a viable, loving relationship.

Sometimes, when life comes undone, it causes us to question the very fabric of our history. Suddenly, everything in our memory is suspect. *Did we really feel the rush of stolen kisses and budding romance? Did we imagine or misinterpret the meaning of all those sweet nothings told to us by our George Baileys?*

We were there. We know that it was real; that it was wonderful! It's so typical, in the heat of a marital battle, to let it be said otherwise. Let nothing slung at you (or allow the temptation to sling it yourself) be received to the contrary. Love cannot be disqualified in reverse. You know it when you feel it. And though it can become damaged along the way, love is a dynamic, living element of our creation. God loved us into existence, and it is love that binds us to Him and to each other.

Once upon a time, life *was* magic. For me, the blessings of our family wrapped around each of us, held us close, and kept us safe as if within a warm blanket. It was enough, in those days, to be thriving in this simple, steadfast bond. We didn't need fancy dinners out. Hotdogs and a box of mac and cheese was gourmet to us because we were together with our family. I believed in us. In my heart, we were among the lucky ones who could say with all honesty, "We had it all."

Fast forward to now, and the overlay of what life has become. The shattering of it all is breathtaking. Even in my sleep, my mind cannot seem to comprehend where the detour happened. All I know for certain is the road no longer has the markings of a place I've ever been before. The faces that I love are still around me, but the blanket that held us bound in contentment, love, and frivolity has been ripped at the seams. Somewhere, between where we began and happily ever after, we got lost.

It is not my interest to levy blame or condemnation, or to distrust at all the memories that blend together and cause us to question what "forever" felt like. When we hear and summarily accept the words spoken over us by men who, within themselves, cannot find the substance to hold on, we feel as though it was all a lie. We even question God as though He is responsible for it falling apart.

God intends for love to grow deeper with age, not for it to fade like the flame that once brought us together. God gives to us the blessings that come with faithfulness, enduring with patience the trials and struggles that everyone has. Among them, there are seasons of plenty and moments that we hold on to and cherish. Contentment is sustainable when we are in alignment with Him.

In the rough patches, laden with burdens and difficulties, God endows us with favor and strength to endure these times. He causes us to persist, to keep walking, to know that He is our Helper and Provider. He yearns for all that we have planted to come to fruition through our children, our grandchildren, our work, and our relationship with each other. What we sow, we reap in a life well lived.

Grey hair is a crown of splendor; it is attained
by a righteous life. (Prov. 16:31)

There is, as we know, a natural progression to life; and with each season, we gain new understanding and perspective that causes us to appreciate what He has given us. When we live a life of gratitude, our gifts and blessings are discovered sometimes in retrospect. We think and remember how God brought us through, giving us moments of great joy. We recall how the difficult times shaped us, sometimes even for the better. As long as He is with us, we will come to know His blessings even in the trials.

It's when we seek the exit sign, leaving the path of righteousness, that we endanger what God has for us. We become lost in the mire of broken expectations and think it is God's fault, or at the very least, our spouse's. So we go looking for happiness elsewhere.

It is overwhelming, standing now in this gaping place and looking back, trying to mend the memory of where things came undone. As if with needle and thread, we attempt to sew the torn, patched fabric. There is simply too much to even know where to begin. The task is impossible. There is no way to reconstruct what happened. We must then ask God to mend the brokenness and show us where we must change to mend those broken aspects of ourselves.

God's plan for us is to emulate His love so that we can give it to each other. When we were first married, and our families were thriving, love was unconditional. We messed up; we made up. We forgave each other. Just like He does with us.

I love the image of the man in Psalm 1, whose "delight is in the law of the Lord."

It says that "He is like a tree planted by streams of water, which yields its fruit in season, and whose leaf does not wither. Whatever he does prospers."

As women, I believe this describes perfectly what we are to do as well. I believe this is the product of unconditional love. When we do not let our circumstances dictate how we love, we thrive no matter what.

A tree that is planted by a stream grows to conform to that stream. The water may rise and fall. The stream may bend and narrow, but the roots dig deep, and the trunk bends and shapes itself to the way of the stream. The stream does not conform to the tree. It carries on, unabated. It ebbs and flows, nourishing and sustaining within it many forms of life. The tree thrives in its current, growing stronger and rooted for generations to climb and live among it. There is nothing to suggest that anything could compromise the viability of the tree. It is nurtured by the water, its branches and leaves reaching skyward as it captures the warmth of the sun and air. It has all it needs to sustain it.

There is no way to anticipate the storm. Some storms rage but the tree stands, unyielding. Other storms come and strike the tree, severing it like a lightning bolt through its trunk and rendering it incapable of withstanding the damage. It happens. And like our own lives, there may have been warnings of inclement weather, but who would have thought such a terrible blow could come and destroy what had seemed impenetrable.

These were the questions that I had for God when my husband left: *What about the love, God? Our history? What about our covenant? How can that just suddenly be swept away? What is unconditional love if one can just leave as if there are no strings attached? No roots that held him bound?*

It's often difficult to pinpoint what happened, what caused something upstream to change you, your family, and your life. Dramatic or simple, an event can happen that does not just cut you down, but yanks you from the soil; and you are no longer stable. You feel disconnected from all sustenance. Unconditional love seems like a fairy tale, but it's not supposed to be.

God intends for us to love each other, to nurture and endure life together. There is no escape clause, no money-back guarantee. We were created to be in love for life.

I know that's not the way it looks right now.

It's important that we stay planted in the soil of God's truth. He knows the plans He has for us—to prosper us, to heal us. Though it feels like we have been severed, cut in two, we are not without hope. We must stay in the nourishment of the stream. We must find stability and strength in knowing He will not let us fall. He will sustain us.

It is far more difficult to uproot yourself and think that you can sustain your own life outside His plans for it. Even for a short time, cut flowers will bloom; but once they are no longer connected to the source, the vine, they wither and fall away.

Your husband may be lulled right now into thinking he is flourishing, blooming even. But sin is a poison that will not sustain anything other than to turn it from thriving into death of spirit, of honor, of life itself.

Just as easily, God can replant what has left the soil of His righteousness and cause new life to come into it. He is the God of Resurrection. He breathes upon what is thought to be dead, or merely lost, and restores vitality. It can happen to your husband. It can happen to your marriage. But you cannot fight this battle or even influence it. It is God's to fight. Stay in the nourishing water of the Word.

There is work to do, tending to your own branches, pruning where necessary, and taking stock in knowing that He has you. Root yourself in what you must do to take shelter from this storm. Care for yourself and for your children. Dwell in faith and expectation that even though you don't know how He will do it, God is mending all your broken places.

Faith is not knowing that God can. It's knowing that He will.

He wants for us—even more than we want it for ourselves—to have a love that endures throughout the years. He already knows the ending of the movie. He truly wants us to have a wonderful life!

Stand tall. Dig deep.

Be the tree.

Now to him who is able to do immeasurably more than all we ask or imagine, according to his power that is at work within us, to him be glory. (Eph. 3:20)

3

The Valley of Midnight

THE VALLEY IS THAT place we find ourselves when the hurt is so overwhelming, so bewildering, that we feel we are not only unable to stand but unable to lay down and rest either. We are shell-shocked from what has happened. Our world is spinning, the dust of which has yet to settle. The valley will become familiar terrain for us for a little while, but it is meant for us only to pitch a tent here, not build a house. We are just passing through.

We learn many things in the valley. Although it is easy to condemn this place, what it teaches will transform us. We toughen up here. We gain perspective. We listen with a new acuity for answers to questions we never thought we would ever have to ask: *What is he thinking? What's going to happen next? How could he just leave me without an explanation?*

Answers do come. Not all at once and rarely are they the ones we want to hear. Sometimes they are raw, hurtful responses that spill out when we discover a new truth, a new implausible reality. Like a bitter pill, they sit unsettled in our stomachs. We cannot fathom that this is our life. We are forced to connect dots that we would rather never had to do.

The answers change us. They both harden us to a steely resolve and soften us at the same time. They make us pliable to new possibilities, yet fearful at the prospect of trusting another human being ever again. We are mixed with vulnerability and anxiety—steeped in a readiness to pounce, to protect what is ours. The concepts of forgiveness and grace are foreign to us here. Every nerve is heightened, and we are on edge.

We come to terms with things in the valley. That doesn't mean we understand fully the how's and why's of what has happened, but we are squeezed into this corner where we must contend with it. So much is left unanswered and unsaid. We piece together fragments of a life we knew with the threads of what is left, and we tie a knot and hold on.

We are alone, or so it seems.

It is here that we plead with God to take away the hurt, to soothe us, to make everything return to "normal." The problem is, normal is anything but that, and God seems silent.

There is no nice way to put it. The valley is a lonely, difficult place. Everything about betrayal leaves us hollow and gasping as if we have just been dumped into the deep part of a lake in the middle of winter. You flail about, looking for something to keep you afloat. You need a life jacket, and instead, a twig floats by.

All the while, you pray that you won't go under.

You don't.

You won't.

You manage, somehow, to get to shore, dry off, and get a look at the surroundings. Oddly, it looks like home but feels very different. The valley perches us uncomfortably between the precipice of what was and what will be. We can't decide in which direction to seek our safety or our solace. We just know that we can't stand still. You begin to move, aimlessly at first, but your feet are moving, and you are trying to find the best pathway out of here. You are in survival mode now.

On good days, well-meaning friends and family surround you. You find yourself staring at them across the table as they chat on about something funny that happened at their cousin's wedding last weekend. Then it hits them. Maybe weddings should probably be one of those subjects on the newly formed Forbidden Topic List.

You pat their hand, smiling at their embarrassed expression, as they realize their faux pas. "It's okay," you say with your words, but your eyes reveal how—even the slightest reference to matrimony— feels like a sucker punch to the gut. Nothing they deem funny is hitting you that way right now. It's not their fault. They love you. They are just trying to get your mind off "it."

Your thoughts drift. Naturally, they default to things like, *Oh, he's just getting off work now, and I hope he remembers to get his prescription refilled.*

You can't help it. You just can't.

The kids, if you have them, still require your constant attentiveness; but even as they speak, sharing what is going on in their world, you find yourself looking at them sort of dazed. As if for some odd reason, they are speaking to you in Japanese and wearing kimonos.

"*Mom?* Did you hear what I said? I'm taking that AP Biology class, and I need that new calculator by Thursday."

"Okay. Yes. Sure. Got it." You nod your head and make them think that you are present to the task, but you know—*they* know— you're not. And again, you slide into that zone between crazed bewilderment and the urge to break out in tears.

Nothing makes sense.

Yesterday, you needed to open a new checking account without your husband's name on it. This morning, when you went to the doctor, you simply stared blankly at the receptionist who verified your "emergency contact." You couldn't decide who else to put down, so you left his name where it was.

Everything is inside-out and upside-down. Simple tasks are now so hard, and hard things, like installing new blinds in your daughter's bedroom, become simple. You roll up your sleeves and dive into each project just to prove that you don't need him around to do it for you.

But you do. There are a thousand things you wish he was there for. You just can't afford to "go there" because the spiral happens so fast. It's best not to think.

At night, the ritual is gone. You still brush your teeth and wash your face, but you find yourself staring longer in the mirror, your face weary and older looking, and everything seems to sag. Nothing is prodding you to hurry and jump into bed because you know what awaits you. Slowly, you pull the covers back and slip onto the mattress as if it were a deserted island. That's the way it feels—a deserted island in the middle of the valley.

Over and over, your mind flashes images of him—the *good* him. The one who loved you back. The one whose arms held you. The one who promised until death do you part.

And you note, looking at your phone, that he hasn't called once. Not once.

I remember willing myself to not reach out to that empty space where my husband used to lay. I read. I turned on the TV at all hours just to drown out the silence. I prayed incessantly. *How could he not be here? How could he just walk away from his family? How could he not miss me even just a little bit?*

The questions came in rapid fire. Even in my dozing off to sleep, my dreams tried to reconcile what my heart and head could not. My rest came in fitful doses with eyes closed, but heart racing like a lost child looking for her mommy in the grocery store. In that place of punchy delirium, exhaustion mixed with a near light-headedness, I tell myself a joke, crudely parodying one of our favorite movies, *Airplane.*

Surely, there must be some mistake, and I am going to wake up and find that it was all a nightmare.

The retort comes in the imagined voice of Leslie Neilson. "No, it's not a nightmare. He's gone. And don't call me, Shirley."

Only I'm not laughing.

This is where the rubber meets the road. Everything within you is raging from the trauma of it all. A trauma caused by him—the *bad* him.

In this place, I came to think of ways that I could disengage my mind. I needed a compass to lead me out of the weeds of tortured thoughts and jumbled, harassing images that would not leave my head. Oh the enemy, he is so very clever at hitting us while we are down.

I began, instead of counting sheep, to count my blessings. It was sort of a dual list that began as What He Left Behind and became What God Has Given Me. It was choppy at first. I had to intentionally focus, to calculate. It was awkward, just like standing in front of my cabinet counting out the plates I would need at the table, less one. As if the arithmetic was hard. I had to tease through my thoughts, hold up each identified blessing, and embrace it. It was like coming back to your home after a fire. Each item uncovered, still intact, became an instant treasure. I inventoried everything.

The list began with the names of my children: Emma, Meredith, Cole, Hope. I had a job. Although I did not know how I would support us completely on its wages, I had at least a starting point. My kids and I were healthy. My mom and my brothers cared for me and were in my corner. I had good friends. My car ran. As did my lawn mower, as did my vacuum cleaner, my appliances. I knew how to do things, fix things, manage things.

I wrote down my list. I looked at it, added to it, memorized it, and repeated it like a mantra. *I have all of this and more*, I thought. Though my husband had what he claimed *he* wanted—fun—his list, had he made one, I was certain would be far less substantial.

I had also the distinction of knowing that I had given my all to my marriage and to my husband, despite his accusations and justifications. I knew it. My friends and family knew it, and God. Most of all, God knew it. I am not perfect, but I had weathered many trials to the best of my ability. I gave grace, and I needed it plenty. I knew that I had done all that I could. And, where there was lack, I asked the Lord—and my husband—for forgiveness.

The Lord, at least, granted it to me.

Throughout my life, I recalled so many stories of people that I knew who had divorced. I remember thinking to myself, *I would so much rather be the one who is left than the one who leaves.* Although little did I know then that it would one day happen to me, I recall thinking that the one who leaves bears the responsibility of breaking up the marriage and family. I simply couldn't conceive of an equitable exchange for family. *Nothing could possibly be worth it. Nothing.* I believe I was right about that then, as I know I still am.

Yet here I was with my list of What God Gave Me, and the one with whom I had acquired it, was no longer at my side. It was incomprehensible to me. In those dark moments, counting sheep and counting blessings, I yearned for sleep. I yearned too to hear my husband's key in the door and his footsteps coming up the stairs to say that he realized he had made a big mistake.

I didn't hear it.

What I did hear, however, came in the gentle whisper of another promise. "I am here," the Presence said to me. "I will not leave you nor forsake you." Like before, it was not audible, but it was. It came like a thought, but in braille. I could *feel* it as it impressed itself on my conscience. "I am here."

The Presence calmed me, soothed me, and held me. It took the edges of my desperation and tempered them, allowing me to take a breath. Slowly, I exhaled and felt the anxiety and my restlessness ease once again.

In my heart came this dialogue with the Lord. "It's all going to be okay. I know what I am doing," I heard Him whisper.

Like a child who struggles to regain composure after a fitful cry, I wanted to curl into that Presence, hold it tightly to me, and fall asleep. I stammered, "I don't know how I'm going to do this, God. It hurts so bad."

"I know. But I am here."

"But what do I do? What in the world do I do about this?"

"Nothing," came the Presence, scrolled across the silence.

"But everything is so broken, I am so broken . . . so are the kids."

"I am here."

"What will you do, God? How will you do this?"

"I know what I'm doing."

"But—"

"Shh. I am here."

I still had very tough, emotional moments. But I also had the knowing that the Lord wasn't just looking from his heavenly throne and surveying the damage of what had become my life. He was *with* me. I didn't just know this; I *felt* it.

I still wrote in my journal, scrawling out my prayers. In the shower, I would stifle my weeping so that the kids would not hear me. I still hurt, but I had begun to trust that He would not leave me. More than this, I began to *expect* to see His hand in the form of new answers that would come.

I was not alone after all.

Solace came to me like a buoy to hold on to out there on that lake. He was holding me up, no matter what it looked like around me. He would not let me go under.

Each long night would fall into morning; and each long day rolled back into night. Day in, day out. Days grew into weeks, and weeks into months. So it is in the valley.

The terrain is rough. We keep walking through it, putting one foot and then the other. Sometimes we find we are accelerating ahead, and other times we're slipping back. It takes all our effort. We skin our knees and we adjust our stride, all in an effort to get to a plateau where we can look out and survey the expanse of where we've been and where we're headed.

The valley is the place where we are transformed, where we become something new. Like pottery in the kiln, we take on a hardness that is useful on our trek in this new land. With just the right glazing, the posturing of our hardships into opportunities, we do something that we have possibly not done in a long time. We shine.

Like a lioness, we roar and announce to the world that we intend not to go gently into the night. Our instincts kick in. We become keener, adept at hunting for provision, listening for danger, protecting our young. We take on plans to see ourselves out of our dilemma. We ration; we start our own fires and learn to do with little. We learn to appreciate smaller comforts, all the while keeping our eyes on Him, waiting for daybreak that is sure to come.

The valley is a place we don't ever want to be, but when we climb out of it, we are inexplicably better for it. God cannot keep us from this time because in it, He transfuses us with a sustenance that, like manna, is meant to supply what we need each day. He wants us to rely on Him, to stay focused, to not despair.

How long, Lord? How long will I be in the valley? How long before it gets easier?

The answers are hard to discern. It all depends on how deep our valley is. For some, it may be for forty days; and others, it may feel like forty years. But I know for certain that you will find your way out of it, and when you do, you will be able to see all the blessings you have gathered along the way.

> *See, I am doing a new thing! Now it springs up; do you not perceive it? I am making a way in the wilderness and streams in the wasteland. (Isa. 43:19)*

Miracles happen in the valley too. God puts people on our path who seem to just understand, who extend a hand, who give offerings of love and friendship that feed us, soothe us, give us rest from all the worrying if only for a little while. In countless ways, "coincidences" manifest into favor that has you in the right place at the right time to receive it. It is awe inspiring to see how life unfolds like a flower in bloom. You can't plan for it. It just happens.

You learn so very much here. Simple things like knowing you can assemble bureaus and clean out your garage and paint rooms and take carloads of things to Goodwill on a Saturday. You know how to mow, edge, and replace broken things just like a champ. You are amazed even at yourself, as others are who are watching you. Before you know it, you are making lemonade from all those lousy lemons you were handed.

I still missed my husband in the valley. But as I moved forward, the burden of what I carried with me grew lighter, and so did my heartache.

The Lord is our guide. He sustains us and gives us strength that we otherwise don't know we have.

Like you, I would have done anything to avoid my time in the valley, to not have to go through all that led me to it. Now, I am so grateful for what it taught me. I came out of it standing a little taller, walking a little more purposeful, and heading in a direction that I would never have found had I not been forced to make this journey.

God is an amazing traveling companion.

I pray that your valley is filled with beautiful streams, waterfalls, and rainbows. On the days when your burden is especially weary, keep walking. You will find the exit just up ahead. Lean on Him. He is with you!

> *The Lord is my shepherd, I shall not be in want. He makes me lie down in green pastures, He leads me beside quiet waters, He restores my soul. He guides me in paths of righteousness for his name's sake.*

> *Even though I walk through the valley of the shadow of death, I will fear no evil, for you are with me; your rod and your staff, they comfort me. (Ps. 23)*

4

But This, I Tell You—Guard Your Heart

I KNOW THAT YOU WILL think that I am half mad when I tell you how important it is for you to guard your heart. It's a paradox, to say the least. After all, this is the same heart that has been trampled on. The same one that perhaps has been betrayed, dishonored, and ravaged by the difficulties you now face.

Certainly, given your current state, how can it now be within your power to protect it? Nothing that can happen to you seems to compare with what you have already endured, but hear me. This is the single most important thing you must do outside of submitting your circumstances to God.

It is so easy, when we are in turmoil, to be compelled to do all we can to assuage our hurt. We feel we are justified in airing out our problems, in seeking strategies to shore up our position, our angst, our intentions to fight back and get even. We want to be right, and we want others to know the details of the injustice we have suffered at the hands of our husband's decisions. It's not pity we are seeking, but we feel that if we could just drag someone into the pit of our despair, we will somehow gain a leg up.

We quickly learn, however, that although it helps us momentarily to ease our burden, to let off steam, we are not wholly better off. There are just more people who know about our situation, which in itself could lead to more problems and vulnerability.

This is a difficult chapter for me to write. Not because I don't believe what I am about to share with you, but because I believe it so greatly that I am constrained to not "preach." You see, I have learned all this the hard way; and like a good tour guide, I want to point out for you the dangerous points along the path you are on.

Healing is our destination. What we will talk about here are the things that will prolong our getting there. That is why we must be careful. Nothing is worse than feeling you are finally getting your two feet back on the ground, only to have them swept out from under you again. Such will be the result if we do not pay attention to some basic, spirit-guided principles that God has already given us to ensure that we stay on the right track.

We all need people to talk to. Professional counseling, ministry, good friends, and family are among the many priceless relationships that give us strength, wisdom, and balm for our woundedness. I am sure that without those whom I have sought good counsel, my journey on this road would have been infinitely more difficult.

There is a nuance here of which I must make distinction. Be careful who you seek counsel from. When we are hurting, we can often seek out people who will understand our plight, and among these, there are those whose advice might seem plausible and worthy of your consideration. However, if what they are telling you from their "if I were you, I would" armchairs conflicts with what your more sensible and righteous inclinations tell you, then please heed your instincts. Of course, not every suggestion that comes our way should be acted on.

Everyone knows someone—who knows someone—who has been in our shoes. The friend who has your best interest at heart is not bad or wrong for telling you what they have learned in their marital or relational experience. It's just that some people give advice about doing "the right thing" because they are guided by the Spirit. Others will advise you to do the thing their Aunt Bernice did when she found out her husband was cheating on her with her sister.

Aunt Bernice is in jail now.

There is much advice out there that you can gain from sources that range from Facebook to YouTube, and everything in between. Some of it may be worthy of consideration, but a lot of it is fluff. If you Google "marital help," there are a dozen gurus that will try to sell you their DVD series on breakthroughs in saving your marriage. I mean not to disparage this. There are, of course, some credible and knowledgeable folks out there, and I'm sure that they have helped many.

I am simply saying that unless you trust—I mean *really* trust— the person you are baring your heart to, you may well be subject of advice that is not just ungodly, but downright bad.

In our situations, everything must be tempered through the filter of righteousness. There are no shortcuts on this road and, unfortunately, there are no do-overs. Everything we say, do, and think is subject to what God would have for us. Hurt or not, justified or not, we must live with our own consciences especially when our husbands may well have ditched theirs.

What this means is that God has rules for waging this kind of war. We must be careful that the weapons we use do not end up dishonoring Him and hurting us even more gravely.

I know right now that this may seem counterintuitive. After all, *you* are the one who is hurting. *You* are the one who is left. *You* are the one who not only carry the burdens of home and family, but must also figure out how to carry on financially, practically, and emotionally.

I don't mean to overgeneralize, but by all accounts, your husband is likely unconcerned or is thinking only about that which relates to himself. Sadly, this way of thinking is all too prevalent and adds even greater to your burden.

Our guts and our instincts want us to rise up, to fight fire with fire. We want the men who left us to also know some of the discomforts we now have. It is said that the best defense is a good offense. Suddenly, our senses and personalities go into overdrive. We are incensed, prodded by statements that swirl in our heads: *How dare he! I'll show him!*

This is not a matter of ignoring these emotions and becoming passive. Nor is it simply taking on the position of waiting for the other shoe to drop. I know how it is when we are left bracing for impact as to what comes next. We are on "high alert." There are things that must be done to protect ourselves, perhaps legally, from what has been done to us. What I am speaking of comes not from the arrows slung at us by our husbands, but by those we sling back in response.

Regardless of how justified we feel, and indeed may well be, this is a different level of protection. It is spiritual. We must act, but it is in how we do so that determines if we are aligned with how God wants us to be. When we act outside of this, we are in danger of not only dishonoring Him, but in losing the favor He bestows upon us.

God is our defender. When we take matters solely into our hands, we fight with the rules of engagement that this world offers and not by the fruits of the Spirit. In doing so, our outcomes may win the battle, but not the war. We come out feeling more bloodied and worse for our wear.

Everything that we do must be in alignment with Him. This must be our foundation. It is from this soil that will grow whatever seeds we plant for our future.

What you cultivate in this season determines whether your crops will blossom in blessings or will be choked off. From hard ground is produced thistle, thorns, and more hardship. It is God's heart that you receive in abundance the return of joy and all that He has for you. This simply cannot be done in soil that is cultivated with bitterness, anger, and anxiety.

How can we do this? Through prayerful consideration of what must be accomplished, communicated, or acted upon when dealing with our husbands, and doing so without malice or revenge.

Remember when you were young and a sibling instigated a reaction from you, perhaps took something from you, and you lashed out, hurting them in the process? Your mom or dad likely ran in to intervene, telling you to apologize, even punishing you for your aggression. All the while, your sibling is laughing and taunting you from behind. It wasn't your fault. The admonition was cruel and perverse in that your sibling seemed to have gotten away with something that you were paying the price for.

Obviously, this is a much bigger deal. You may be standing shocked and incredulous at the suggestion that, just like then, you are seemingly powerless; so much comes at you. Blame and innuendos of how *you* are responsible for what *he* has done compels you to respond and defend yourself. With each egregious pitch lobbed, you swing, aiming to hit it out of the park to validate your competence and your worth.

The only problem is, this is a pitch that you will never hit. It's a knuckle ball designed to fake you out.

It's difficult in this season to think of "turning the other cheek," as Jesus taught. However, I believe that the Lord's intention in saying this is to not only confront ill will with a tempered spirit, but to protect us from engaging in the sinful behaviors that breeds contempt. We are called upon to love those who persecute us, calling no distinction between loving only those who love us back. We are to love everyone.

Granted, this does not mean we are to let others walk over us and subject us to whatever derelict or egregious act they desire upon us. What it does mean, however, is that even those who are doing wrong to us are children of God too.

When we resist in conducting ourselves in the same manner, and perhaps reprehensible way we have been treated, we protect ourselves from being outside of God's will.

> *Love your enemies, and pray for those who persecute you . . . He causes his sun to rise on the evil and the good, and sends rain on the righteous and the unrighteous. (Matt. 5:44–45)*

Jesus commanded us to love our neighbors (including those who once lived under our roof) as ourselves. He wants us to love even the unlovable, and especially them. For it is through this that we may be as our Father in heaven and not of the world.

Our husbands fall into this category. No matter what they have done, no matter how much they have hurt us.

There is no doubt that this can be immensely hard to do. How do you rename love for someone who has likely told you that they don't/can't/no longer feel the same? Like the line, "I love you, but I'm not in love with you." It sounds good, but it is simply meaningless.

We do not have to stay in relationship with someone to love them the way that God asks us to. The Bible gives us no qualifiers. Jesus simply says to "love one another." In so doing, we must question every action we take, every word we say, and filter it through His Word. We *must* love. It doesn't matter what your husband says and does. What matters is what *you* say and do. You can only control you.

As for your man who left, God will deal with him directly. He doesn't need your help in reminding Him of all the terrible things that have occurred. The Lord knows all. Remember, your husband did not just walk away from you. He walked away from Him too. Whether your husband finds his way back to you or not, pray that he comes back to God. That's what love does.

The opposite of this is ugly.

It is hard, in the face of injustice, to not want to lash out, but an "eye for an eye" never solves anything. It only blinds us. It causes the cycle of hurt and retribution to go on indefinitely. It causes our soil to harden, and from it, nothing good can grow.

Soon sprouts of bitterness and unforgiveness take root. People go to their grave with these toxic emotions, and they can continue for generations. God does not want that to happen to us. We must guard our hearts, and our spirits, of any such thorns before they overtake us.

The challenge is that your husband is likely not playing by the same rules. Things he says and does are all meant to incite you, to put you off guard, to even cause you to react in such a way to prove that it is you, not him, who is the crazy one. All of this, of course, is to serve his need to illustrate why his reasoning for leaving you was sound.

We well know the ploy of the enemy and his willing minions to create diversions and operate in untruths. This is how he ropes us in. This is how he keeps the sabotage alive so that the light of truth and accountability cannot shine forth and create a bridge by which a peaceful truce can be made.

Anger and resentment drive us to say and do things that we could never imagine of ourselves. You are in the fight of your life, and in this, you feel compelled to speak out, to defend yourself, to make it known that the blame for what has happened must be laid at your husband's feet, not yours. After all, he is the one who caused all of this, not you. Right?

The problem here is that he, your husband, is not the only one who is guilty. Jesus taught, "If a blind man leads a blind man, both will fall into a pit."

If you have tried, as I did, to respond to your husband's every accusation and unreasonable declaration, then you know the terminal frustration of doing so. There is absolutely no way to win this argument. None. It doesn't matter how absurd the contention is that he has laid before you; it is a useless proposition to even begin to explain the contradiction to his points. Anything you say is irrelevant to him. He is unwilling to hear any opposition to what he has convinced himself. No matter what you say, even if you are *agreeing* with him, it will not be received as valid.

At this stage, even your history together becomes contorted, manipulated, edited, and revised. Suddenly, despite his seeming inability to remember important dates or sweet things you used to do together, he now has supersonic, laser-like memory and precision at naming things that happened twenty years ago that he never forgot. Every time you mismatched his socks or were even the slightest insensitive to his attention comes flooding back like the breaking of a dam. There are things that he has said of you that, if true, even *you* wouldn't like you. But honestly, this is all part of the initial stage. You can't receive any of this as truth. It is deception at its best.

Like a rocket being sent into space, the expulsion that must be created to launch requires the consumption of all energy to propel it. The goal is to get the rocket into orbit, and in so doing, must separate the rocket from the payload so that it can enter space where the pull of gravity does not hold it bound. The vehement, almost monster-like attributes your husband may employ are similar. He is fueled by any means necessary to achieve the objective of propelling him into his own stratosphere without you. His mission is selfishly devised to allow him to explore new frontiers, which he has convinced himself to be happier places to orbit.

This requires intensity to all resistance with the cold, hard reality of creating the divide that will jettison him forward so that there is no uncertainty of his intentions. Whether his objectives were well thought out or not, he intends only one thing—to act as decisively as necessary so that he could convince, not only you, but himself, that there be no margin for misinterpretation.

When my husband announced that he was leaving, we had a room in our garage that he had built for one of our young-adult children. He moved in there for several weeks as he prepared to vacate our home and our marriage completely. During this time, it was if a stranger had come and invaded his body. He didn't even look like the same man. He came, went, argued, and defied every aspect of our relationship. The more rebellious and emphatic that he was in living his "own life," the more desperate I became to refute what spewed from him. I wanted so very much to find the crack in his new demeanor.

I begged. I pleaded. I cried in near hysterics. Nothing penetrated his defiance.

When appealing to his heart and emotions failed, I decided the only way forward was to go toe-to-toe with him. On every point, I shot back a counterpoint. The uglier he was, the uglier I got. Then language, and words that I abhor most, were being sent like missiles around the common areas of our home. The kitchen became a war zone.

Soon, an odd transformation happened in me. A latent, "truck driver" mouth grew from my spine, and I was lobbing every colorful phrase and innuendo right back at this man who, for thirty years of my life, I had adored and cherished. That's what sheer panic and chaos will do to an otherwise normal, good woman.

It's a funny thing. Despite how despicable it got, even though I was "holding my own" against him, I felt even more despondent than before. Not only was my husband someone that I no longer recognized, but so was I.

It was not long before he left without even a goodbye. He was successful in his attempt to paint me as unstable, and himself as doing the only reasonable thing a man could do in his shoes—leave. He was flush with victory and a new life, and I was left holding the shattered pieces of everything else.

This is not to say that, had I acted more out of love, more in line with the edicts of my faith, that it would have changed the outcome. I am beyond certain that my husband was bent on leaving no matter what. However, the heartache of knowing that I descended to the depths of depravity by taking the bait and allowing myself to react with such emotional volatility bothers me still. Despite what had become our issues, I deeply loved this man; and when he left, the legions of hell were rejoicing at the chaos they had caused.

This is a scar that only time, and God, can take away.

Jesus taught, "What goes into a man's mouth does not make him unclean, but what comes out of his mouth, that is what makes him unclean." It is from our mouths that what is in our hearts is revealed. This is how we sin. This is how we give the enemy a foothold and allow anything we say and do to create even greater hurt, shame, and disrespect. These injuries take us completely out of alignment with God; and in this way, the enemy is vindicated, not us.

We must stand, therefore, in truth. We must heed the instruction of God to withstand the impulse to act outside of love. To love even when it hurts. To stand righteously and turn the other cheek so that He can fight our battles for us.

I honestly believe that men who leave marriages absolutely are compelled to justify their actions. In so doing, they must paint the picture that life with you warranted their departure. They must convince others, and themselves, that leaving was the only sensible thing to do.

That is on them, not us. They will have to live with that, just like I've had to reconcile the way I fought to defend myself instead of letting God do it for me.

All we can do is go forward.

As we guard our hearts, do so in humility and grace. Remove the rancor and the retribution from the tone of our voices. Stop texting the digs, the shaming, and the sarcasm that only serve to rake flaming coals onto our husbands' laps, as if that alone will cause them to be kind and become the men they used to be. As if by some stroke of magic, they delight in our barbs and will suddenly love us again. It doesn't work. Instead, it only stokes the fire hotter and burns whatever remains of the relationship to the ground.

God would have us love in the manner of being kind. He wants us to find comfort in Him and to trust that He is working all things meant for evil for our good.

When it comes to communicating with our men, simply "let your 'yes' be 'yes,' and your 'no,' be 'no'; anything beyond this comes from the evil one."

I know how difficult this is. It may take practice. Pray. Ask the Lord to help you so that you can operate on the level of doing what God wants of us. When you remove the wood from the fire, it goes out. Let's not allow anything else that comes from our mouths, or our actions, give more fuel to the enemy or our husbands. This alone can open the door to building bridges of all kinds.

If you make a mistake and have a setback—and you will—forgive yourself and do better next time. Keep working at it.

Healing is our destination.

Love one another even in the most impossible and devastating circumstances. Even if you can't bring yourself yet to act in kindness or humility for your husband, then do it for Him. Do it for yourself, your children, and your future. Till your soil, and your harvest will be abundant of all that is good. You have much to reap. Sow wisely.

Guard your heart.

But the fruit of the Spirit is love, joy, peace, patience, kindness, goodness, faithfulness, gentleness and self-control. (Gal. 5:22–23)

Above all else, guard your heart, for everything you do flows from it. (Prov. 4:23)

Keep your mouth free of perversity; keep corrupt talk far from your lips. Let your eyes look straight ahead; fix your gaze directly before you. Give careful thought to the paths of your feet. (Prov. 4:24–26)

5

Mirror, Mirror on the Wall

WE HAVE TALKED ABOUT the woundedness, about the grieving that happens to us in this process of finding that we are suddenly on our own. It's easy to look at our lives and see the parts of us that need healing. There are pieces of us strewn here and there that require mending, fixing, reorganizing. Everything still feels a bit clunky, unnatural, and fitted together as if by duct tape and string. We are downsizing, not just our physical surroundings, but also our expectations, our dreams, our identities.

We feel that every way we turn requires us to reorient some aspect of ourselves.

Like a square peg in a round hole, it's like we are hovering, trying to decide how to land so that we are somewhat less conspicuous than we feel. If only we could camouflage ourselves. Instead, we come and go. We do our shopping and head to work. We take care of our responsibilities, our kids, our parents, our friends, while we still show up to life events when and where we are supposed to. So what if that smile on our faces is a bit crooked and painted on. We're there, right?

Or are we.

It's interesting how battered our identities become. We used to look in the mirror and be reasonably satisfied with our appearances, knowing that the laugh lines around our eyes and mouths were put there by our experiences, our good times, the love we shared. Though fatigued and weary, we muddled through with an extra dab of moisturizer or some fancy cover-up that the lady at the cosmetic counter suggested would take years off our looks.

It was all good.

I was proud of these markings, these wrinklings. They were like tiny roadmaps that led directly to my soul. They spoke for me of what held me together—love and family and grace. Somehow, they added to my appearance, showing depth and resiliency of a life well lived. Even on my worst bad-hair day, I looked reasonably happy. And I was.

Then *it* happened.

The toll registered right away as if on the Richter scale; the foundation of my life shifted. I noticed at once that as I stared at the reflection before me, I resembled the "old" me, but didn't at the same time. Something was missing. As if the mirror possessed a new filter through which I could see myself, it was unnerving. My whole countenance had changed, and not in a good way.

You can tell a lot about a person when you look into their eyes. What I had once considered my "normal" appearance seems downright carefree as I think about it now. It was enlightened by the fact that my eyes held validation, joy, respect, gratitude for my blessings. Much of what they held came from the reflection of my husband's value of me as his wife. I felt I belonged to him. I felt cherished, and it showed.

Once he left, and the dust of reality started to settle that he was not intending to come back anytime soon, that changed almost overnight. The woman standing before me in the mirror was a dull and empty version of myself.

If that wasn't enough, the enemy was hard at work, convincing me of some new labels by which to call myself. "Unworthy," "unlovable," and when he was really getting my goat came the whopper—"damaged goods." Certainly, I concurred, if my own husband no longer felt that life with me was appealing, what hope was there? I was doomed for sure.

There is this annoying game we used to play as kids called, I Know You Are But What Am I? I'm sure you recall it. No matter what your friends or siblings would verbally toss your way to label you, such as a cheater, a goof ball, a thumb-sucking baby, it didn't matter. You could simply retort, "I know you are but what am I?" and the frustration would cycle around and around until everybody just gave up and went home.

This game resurrected itself in adulthood for me specifically when my husband was bailing ship. Every statement I pronounced in his direction, every rhetorical question I lobbed to get him to think about the consequence of what he was doing, came whizzing back at me like an aced tennis shot that you are hopeless to ever return.

"I know you are blaming me, but you're the one who—"

On and on and on. Nothing registered; nothing made sense. Nothing came back with an effective, thoughtful response. Just zingers and whizzes that hurt when they landed, and they always did.

I could have saved myself a ton of extra hardship and counseling had I thought ahead and realized that I could not reason with this mentality. It was impossible to do so. Instead, I took it. All the while, my husband was racking points and standing proudly under the scoreboard, winning the war of words. Using this tactic requires very little skill, but it is efficient in getting us to shut up and sit down on the sidelines while he is busy grandstanding.

My husband soundly defeated my every concept that this was going to end well. He drew blood, metaphorically, and from that seeped out all that had been reflected in my once happier gaze.

Just like that, our husbands seem able to withdraw their love, protection, covenant, and validation. We, on the other hand, become for a brief time, nearly lifeless, as though we must acclimate to an atmosphere that is without sufficient oxygen. We are hardly moving, barely able to recognize ourselves at all. We are in shock.

I think that there is a secret society of men who pledge, should they exit their marriages, that they will do so while leaving no trace of humanity, no kindness, no hope for reconciliation. I think it's a pact that they sign. They *decide*. They make a cut that separates their former life from the one they are pledging as the one they've "always truly wanted." It makes you wonder—what do they see when *they* look in the mirror?

If your spouse was anything like mine, then he became an instant primping pro. Hair products, teeth whiteners, and new smells from colognes that you know were not tied up with ribbon under last year's Christmas tree, all take up space around his sink. Overnight, the transformation of your man of sensible sensuality happens; and you stare wide-eyed at his attempt to recreate a younger, wealthier-looking version of himself. Suddenly, GQ and Men's Health are his favorite magazines, and you are sure, judging by his new look, that he truly believes the saying, "Clothes make the man."

Before, you could barely get him to take a multi-vitamin. And now, supplements with names you can't even pronounce line your kitchen counter.

He sees only what he wants to see about himself in the reflection. A skin-deep persona that he is suddenly someone special, a great catch for some lucky gal that will *truly* appreciate him, a Good Time Charlie; and you are the only one who knows he's gone bad. According to all reports, there exists a universe of people who are applauding his newfound freedom.

What could go wrong?

While he is spit shining his shoes, dancing his way into his new life, you are in your slippers, your eyes and nose red, and feeling that you are a much older, much poorer version of the gal you used to be.

I don't care what gets reported back to you or how happy he suddenly seems. A man simply cannot change his true colors like a chameleon and not expect remnants of the real man to come bleeding through, like the colored undershirt he's wearing underneath his new slim-fitting white button down. It's going to come out somehow. He can party like it's 1999. Not everyone is going to believe his story that he's a contender for Sexiest Man Alive. When the rooster crows three times and he denies that he knows you, it's going to hit him eventually.

If you look real close at those Instagram pics, his gaze will reveal what his face and words will not. He's having fun, all right, but his eyes reflect the condition of his soul. "The eye is the lamp of the body. If your eyes are good, your whole body will be full of light," Jesus said in Matthew 6:22.

Your man is barely a tiki torch in broad daylight.

It is important to remember too that just as the enemy is feeding us baloney about our identities, he is doing the same to our husbands. In their minds, they are gulping down the lies that he is feeding them just like a hotdog-eating contest in July. Everything is hunky dory, and there is no consequence when life is so merry.

But there is. There always is.

My grandmother used to say, "When you dance, you've got to pay the fiddler." Our husbands just haven't gotten the bill yet.

For all our disappointment, we already have come to understand a fundamental truth: the only one we can truly trust is God. What He says, goes. The devil may be having a field day, but when it comes down to it, the price that is paid for sin will last longer than a sour stomach overstuffed with Oscar Meyer wieners. A man can lose all he has before he realizes the price he paid. Just like Esau selling his birthright for a bowl of beans, it seems like a good idea at the time.

Knowing this doesn't help us. Our emotions are on full tilt. We are angry, hurt, sad, and disillusioned at the betrayal.

In our darkest moments, God sends us His spirit. He speaks to us not just through His Word, but also in others who show up at just the right moment, offering us encouragement and solace. He knows what we need. Although He cannot take from us our burden, He has a purpose for it. It will shape us and define us in ways that we cannot yet imagine, and it will be for good.

Though we may not feel it, God tells us that we are still beautiful.

> *To bestow on them a crown of beauty instead*
> *of ashes, the oil of gladness instead of mourning, and*
> *a garment of praise instead of a spirit of despair.*
> *(Isa. 61:3)*

I like this image *so* much better than the one that greeted me as I stared zombie-like in my sweats and no makeup.

Thankfully, God does not care about our outward appearance. He cares about the conditions of our hearts. Though our eyes may be downcast, He is the lifter of our heads. He is not impressed by fancy clothes or newfound charisma. He cares about our faithfulness, our righteousness, and whether we love Him, and each other, as we love ourselves.

We cannot always be complete in what He desires for us. We fall. We sin. We doubt. We hurt others and we get hurt.

But He wants us to see the way *He* sees us. With love. With compassion. With mercy and grace.

> *You turned my wailing into dancing, you*
> *removed my sackcloth and clothed me with joy that*
> *my heart may sing to you and not be silent. (Ps.*
> *30:11–12)*

Too often, instead of giving God our troubles, we turn to idols. We anesthetize our sorrows by changing our living arrangements, our looks, our habits; and we think we are fooling others into believing that we are doing well. We may fool some, we may even fool ourselves, but God knows.

He wants us to repent, to turn back to Him and to righteousness. This is where we get to find true joy and happiness again.

He stands, waiting for us, no matter how long it takes.

> *Humility and the fear of the Lord are riches*
> *and honor and life. (Prov. 22:3)*

It's interesting, when you think about the mirror, that what we look at as we regard our reflection is actually an inverted image. In other words, our right-sided features actually *appear*, when facing back at us, to be our left. Our brains have made the leap of 180-degree conformity, and we are naturally able to make the opposing, proper placement without difficulty.

The mirror can also cause us to see an imagined comparison of ourselves against an invisible standard that we think our appearances should be like. When we are hypercritical of our looks, our weight, our double chins, we adjust our assessment downward so that we are a lesser version of ourselves when compared to others.

We do the same with our marriages. We look for things that are wrong; we grossly overanalyze its condition. We discount and distrust what God has given us as not being worth holding on to, and we begin to seek options.

Pride is a false reorientation of our hearts. It tells us that *we* come first. That *our* happiness is most important. We roll our eyes at the absurdity our marriages have become without ever evaluating what we have contributed to the cause. "Pride comes before a fall," the Proverbs warn.

God knows the condition of our hearts. Even when we are wearing bright, shiny trinkets and driving fancy new cars. He knows our thoughts, our desires, and whether we love ourselves more than those He has given to us to love.

The mirror can tell us if we need a haircut and whether we've applied our eyeliner appropriately. It can assure us of our appearance and encourage our self-esteem when we need a boost in a new outfit for a big interview. It will confirm for us when our countenance is weary, tired, or sad. It will even lie to us when we ask if we are the fairest of them all.

But beauty—real beauty—is not only skin deep.

Real beauty is reflected from the inside out. It's the reflection of our hearts. It's how we love. It's choosing to be faithful, to stand for covenants, to do what is right even when it's hard. It's believing for the best even when there is no evidence for it.

Even in our brokenness, we should never count out what God can do. If He could raise Lazarus from the dead, He can raise us up also. Know that God can see what we cannot. Know that He sees well into our future and that He already has fixed what is broken and mended what matters most.

Now faith is being sure of what we hope for and certain of what we do not see. (Heb. 11:1)

Don't trust the image that looks back at you. Neither should you trust the images that come, intended to celebrate your husband's newly chosen life. Nothing is truly as it seems.

Of course, you know that Facebook is not *The Book*. You know also that not all that glitters is gold. Fool's gold, maybe.

The fiddler is coming, and he always gets paid.

As you stare at your reflection, remember what it is that God says of you and how He holds you in your naked despair. Let nothing that the enemy lobs at you, stick. Let it whiz past you, just like the lie that it is. If that doesn't work, you only need to ask one thing of the devil: "I know you are, but what am I?"

And to put on the new self, created after the likeness of God in true righteousness and holiness. (Eph. 4:24)

Or do you not know that your body is a temple of the Holy Spirit within you, whom you have from God? (1 Cor. 6:19)

For we are God's masterpiece created to do good things that He has planned for you to do long ago. (Eph. 2:10)

It's like trying to gather up feathers on the ground. You sweep them up into a little pile, only to find the breeze scattering them again—impossible to hold down or contain. Everything is changing. Everything. And it is scattered in directions to and fro, and without rhyme or reason. Nothing makes sense anymore. Yet I'm supposed to "move on." From the author's journal

6

Limbo

FORGIVE ME IF WHAT I say here seems as though I am back-sliding a bit. That's not my intention. I do not want to offer anything that would hinder your progress and healing, but I would be remiss if I did not spend a few pages shining a light on this place because I believe it is one you are likely dealing with as well. While doing all we can to shore up our emotions, it follows us around like a shadow, and it wreaks havoc from time to time.

Limbo is a place we visit along the road to recovery. It's not a place we want to stay in. In fact, I suggest that we spend as little time as possible here. But it is one we must pass *through* so that we get to the other side of it.

One definition of limbo is defined by the Catholic religion as "the border place between heaven and hell." Although I don't ascribe to the belief that such a place exists, I would say, metaphorically, that the limbo I am talking about has similar qualities. It's that place between hurt and healing. It's mid-center point where the hemorrhaging of your emotions has slowed, but you still can't watch a

Hallmark commercial without a box of tissues close by. The dumbest things still set you off, and you can't, for the life of you, figure out why.

There is an old Glen Campbell song, "Everybody's Talkin'," that has stuck with me all these years.

Everybody's talking at me
I don't hear a word they're saying
Only the echoes in my mind
People stop to starin'
And I can't see their faces
Only the shadows of their eyes.

We survived the initial trauma to our lives when our husbands left, and we have managed thus far to not end up in the funny farm. Our stamina is coming back. We push ourselves, wanting to show the world that we are now steady on our feet. With a little extra concealer under our eyes to hide the circles and learning to stand a little taller, we are able to pull off faking it 'til we make it. In fact, we are almost good at it.

We're supposed to be "moving on," as though there is some magical timeline that we need to follow. As if there is an ambiguous milestone, a graduation of sorts, awaiting us or acceptance into a club for Women Without Husbands.

People tell us, "You are doing great!" or "I can't believe how well you look! See? Everything always works out for the best!"

I wanted to beat those people up.

To us, the walking wounded, it's more accurate to say that we feel we should be awarded a Medal of Valor or a Purple Heart. We are survivors of a battle we did not wish to engage in. We hide our hurts and nurse them the best we can while no one is watching. These are scars that we will carry for the rest of our lives, and no one better tell us otherwise. They are our badges of honor.

I wish I could tell you where the point is on the road that designates when we turn the corner. That point where the scale tips and we have more good moments than difficult ones. Or where it is that we discover exactly what it is we want and which direction to head in to find it. But from what I can tell, we round one bend, only to find there are more up ahead. How I wish we could bypass this part of the journey or somehow make a detour around it.

We can't.

To recover fully, our spiritual GPS will have us constantly "rerouting" until we get where we need to be. Short of that destination, we cheat the process and end up bringing all that has yet to heal with us into our new seasons.

Limbo is the place where we empty all our emotions so that God can fill us up again.

Even now, to keep my mind occupied while going through difficult times, I listen to sermons, audio books, worship songs, and even the Bible through my headphones at night. Anything to lull me to sleep steeped in the Word. As if preparing for a hurricane, I utilize whatever I can, like sand bags bolstering my mind, my heart, and my spirit against the storm.

Run off, however, still occurs. Sadness still seeps in. Listening to good stuff helps, but it is only one weapon in our arsenal. We must use everything we can to reinforce our healing.

Intermixed with these nurturing audio inputs are the voices of friends and family who gently try to prod us on our path by imparting their pearls of wisdom. There is plenty of persuasion as to how to release the tethers that still bind us to a man who has long left the scene. All are offered in a sincere effort to help, but sometimes, they all blend together.

I reached a place where the pressure got too much.

After a while, the cacophony of advice hit me, and I was unable to filter what I needed to hear from what I should discard. All of it seemed to compete, informing me what I *should* do, how I *should* feel, and how much better my life would become now that I was "free." I was being escorted down a road I didn't want to be on, yet I had to be.

I came to a breaking point and realized I needed to turn off the highway and idle for a bit. I needed to hear God. I felt as though I was working overtime to corral my feelings, making myself feel a certain way when, underneath, I was not ready. Like herding cats, my emotions, my deepest thoughts and prayers, all scattered and flowed back to a place where I knew the greatest peace.

If I were to be audited by a counselor, I may not be sanctioned in the thoughts I offer, but this is *my* experience. This is *my* story. If I am to write from the place of integrity, then I must offer here what is my truth.

Despite all the evidence against it, despite all the toxic emotions that had built up at the end of our time together, I still wanted a miracle for my marriage. I wanted to still believe that God could turn us around and that all the work I had done to let go was no longer necessary.

I'm not sure if that which we cling to, the remnants of relationship, the seeds that were sown in the soil of promised harvest, can be so easily clipped. With our hands to the plow, we aren't supposed to look back. We're supposed to carry on, facing forward onto the path that God puts us on in faith.

Everything we ever wanted is what we thought He had already ordained. It was defined in our covenant with a man we believed carried the righteousness to remain on the path with us. A man we counted on to hold us, to cherish us, to love us forever. Therefore, we look back; and like Lot's wife, we have moments where we feel ourselves turning to pillars of salt.

Limbo is the fork in the road.

These moments—or hours, or days—conveniently happen alongside the "firsts." The first birthdays, the first Thanksgiving, Christmas, and Valentine's Day. The first anniversary of when you met, got engaged, got married. The firsts will take you out to the woodshed and beat you to a pulp. There is no antidote for it, no way to escape it hitting you squarely in the center of your chest.

You can't pretend your way through it.

Doubt and sadness come back around and will hit you every time you realize that you are with friends and family but are the only one who is not part of a couple. Or when you attend the baby shower for a coworker, and everyone is talking about funny things that happened when their babies were born and how their husbands still do sweet things on Mother's Day.

It's death by a thousand paper cuts.

The remedy is found on the head of a pin. It's so precarious, so unsteady, that you never quite feel you have managed to stand without wobbling. It is the place where you are neither where you were, or where you are supposed to be.

We ask aloud, "God, where are you?"

We wait in anticipation for Him to show us a glimpse of what our outcome will be. We seek, desperate for a sign that He will not let us fall as we sit precariously, like a trapeze artist suspended in air. We need to be convinced that God sees where we are and has not forgotten us.

He hasn't.

> *"For I know the plans I have for you," declares the Lord. "Plans to give you hope and a future."* (Jer. 29:11)

To hasten my trek through this place, I would force myself to think of all the red flags, all the numerous infractions my husband presented, both in our marriage and during our "uncoupling." Literally, I would write in my journal lists of things that happened, times of incredible hurt and disbelief at how callous he had become. There was plenty to choose from. Things I had tucked away, forgiven and forgotten, but there nonetheless. It helped for a little while, as if peeking beneath the tarp that covers our former lives allows us some perspective of the distance we have come.

When we look at the expanse of our uncertain future, that we are alone in uncharted territory, the urge to run backwards comes on us so strong that it throws us into a fit of gloom. This is where those petulant questions pick at our wounds: "How am I ever going to meet someone who will love me?" "Who will understand me? Find me funny? Charming? Smart? A good cook?" "Who could love me like he used to?" "How can I ever love anyone as much as I loved him?"

We wonder if we should come wrapped with a description of ourselves for our next prospective mate: One Not-So-Gently-Used Woman, High Miles but Runs Good.

No wonder the man who left us is the only one we think we still deserve. Our hearts, broken as they are, still want what they used to know.

The problem is that "backward" is a place that is taped off like a crime scene. We're not supposed to go there when we are "moving on." Yet like an obstinate child, our hearts leave the grasp of reason and run back. Our minds—for just a hot minute—linger, scanning the possibility that somehow, someway, our husbands might ride back in and, with a repentant heart and a transformed spirit, want to make everything right.

It does happen. It *could* happen.

I know the danger in thinking like this. I know too how against sound judgement this seems. Most of whom I trust and listen to would deflect this thinking as not being sage. It does not bode well for my emancipation from the destruction my husband left in his wake. But I am writing about hearing God.

My point is not to abandon the journey of seeking out your next season in faith that God will take you to it. He will. It is simply that you let *Him* take you there.

I have found that in my rush to get to my new season, I have gotten ahead of God a bit. Emotionally, I censor what I feel because "I shouldn't feel that." "I need to let go." "I need to stop thinking about him." And that is all true.

I think that I have to push myself out there. I tell myself that I need to think like a soon-to-be divorced woman: "How and where can I meet good, God-loving, eligible men? What do I need to do to be the woman that will attract a nice man?"

All of this, though practical, is not helpful. I am emotionally nowhere near ready for this. Yet the world thinks I should be.

If I am to listen deeply to my spirit, what if God is also saying, "Hold on. Is this what *you* say or what *I* say? Is this what others are telling you? Or *me?*"

Limbo is a place of many questions and few, if any, answers.

I know that you, like me, are climbing out of a pit. You are trying to find your footing. You are using every ounce of energy to get up and out of it so that you can rebuild. All of this is absolutely necessary. None of what will come with this is bad. This is not an attempt to kick up more dirt or push you down again.

What I am saying is that I think that the world would have us running up the steps like Rocky Balboa, arms up in victory as we show we are pumped and ready to rumble, when our hearts aren't possibly there yet. This is one hundred percent okay.

Naturally, we want others to see that we are strong, able to take the hits and no longer backed into a corner of the ring. But what if God, who does our fighting for us, wants us to consider that we lower our fists, just sit for a while, and watch Him do for us what we can't do for ourselves. What if He has a different ending? What if there is a truce that we simply didn't see coming? What if He is not done with our story yet?

He isn't.

Regardless of the outcome, God will reveal to us His purpose for taking us down a particular path all in His time.

> *"I make known the end from the beginning."*
> *(Isa. 46:10)*

We are so anxious to find a point to focus on, an outcome, that we go headlong in that direction. We express our intention; we enter the compass coordinates of where we think we are supposed to land and go full speed ahead. There is nothing wrong in this thinking. It delivers us in that intended vicinity, and we achieve progress.

But sometimes, we lose sight of the horizon. We sail on our own steam and arrive at a place that we did not fully intend. Worse than this, God did not intend for us.

Like tuning a radio station too far from the tower, we get lots of static. It is hard to hear. We are distracted. Find the clearest signal, the one closest to what your heart is telling you to listen and cut out the distortions as best as you can. I say your *heart* because if you are truly listening to it, it will be in sync with your spirit. It will be in tune with God.

Sometimes, that means doing nothing. It means waiting. It means tuning in to the higher frequency of what He is doing in our midst. It's keeping your eyes on the weather and waiting on Him to direct us which way to go.

Taking one path over another will not always work out as our deepest yearnings want. But when we want only His will for our lives, His outcome, we will land in exactly the place we are intended to land. This always turns out to be the *best* one for us.

I remember asking someone during a particularly difficult day, "Does it take more faith to believe for what looks like the impossible? For God to reach my husband, turn his heart of stone back into flesh, and believe for reconciliation? Or does it take more faith to just believe that I will be okay when this season is over?"

The answer, I believe, is that *all* that we hope for requires trusting Him. We must be open to an outcome that is not a product of our forcing our way through this knothole, but letting us be guided through it. No matter what, if it is God's will for us, the evidence will be in our faith. There is a miracle being produced right now behind the scenes that will be a testimony of what God is doing on our behalf even when we are uncertain of what that is.

We can listen to the best sermons, go to the best counselors, and inundate ourselves with teachings of every kind. We can take all the practical steps toward independence, achieving many solid milestones and establishing our fortitude as one who has overcome many obstacles that this season has presented us.

To God be all the glory for every new pinnacle reached.

These are all landmarks of Limbo.

In this place, my prayers for my husband did not change. I prayed, constantly, that he would hear God. I prayed that he would be redeemed, reconciled to Him, for his sake and for my children. And in the deepest recesses where words do not form but my spirit groans, I prayed that he would reconcile with me too.

Does this mean that I expect it? Does this mean that all the evidence that points to it never happening does not exist? All it means is that I want God to decide what happens, not me.

If you have already passed beyond this possibility in your heart, then that is God. If you still have a flicker of hope that He is doing something despite what everyone is telling you that you must do to cut the cord, then I believe that is God too.

In speaking with a pastor, a member of my family whom I trust and whom I know has my best interest in mind, I heard his heart when he said, "The world will always tell you there is no hope, but if God has not fully released your heart, He has a purpose for that. When He releases you, you will know it. And if He hasn't released you yet, there is a reason for that also. He has a purpose for all that He does."

If there is a take away here, it would be summed up like this: We must keep walking. We must keep trusting that God is leading us in the direction we need to go. If we believe that God is good, if we stand in knowing that He alone knows the end of our story, then He will provide us miracles. He will heal us. He will provide restitution through our victory in our new season, whatever that looks like.

No one will have to tell you when you are in limbo. You will know beyond a shadow of a doubt. However, it may take you a while to know that you have left it. God will give you glimpses of it. Your heart and spirit will come gradually to know that the path you are on *is* the right one. You know, deep down inside, what you are believing for.

Don't talk yourself into or out of one way of being. Listen to your heart. There is no wrong or right answer. There is only what He wants for us.

I'm goin' where the sun keeps shinin'
Through the fallin' rain
Going where the weather suits my clothes
Bankin' off the northeast winds
Sailin' on a summer breeze
Skippin' over the ocean like a stone.
("Everybody's Talkin'" by Harry Nilsson)

Trust in the Lord with all your heart and lean not on your own understanding; In all your ways acknowledge him, and he will make your paths straight. (Prov. 3:5–6)

7

Under the Bed

I DON'T KNOW ABOUT YOU, but when I was growing up, the issue of monsters was not a big one. The scariest movie I ever saw as a child was The *Wizard of Oz*. Although the wicked witch and the flying monkeys frightened me some, I don't recall ever having trouble going to sleep because I feared that they were lurking underneath my bed. My imagination just didn't go there.

What I feared the most was being left somewhere and unable to find my way home. Or worse, the imagined finality of my mother or grandmother dying. That tormented me. They were the ones who held my world together at that stage of my life. They were my security blanket. Thankfully, my grandmother lived well into my thirties; and my mom, now close to eighty, still runs circles around me. But as a young girl, just the thought of something happening to either one of them was enough to cause me anxiety.

As for my dad, he and my mom divorced when I was six, and he spent the next several years disengaged from my brothers and me. It's an unfortunate tale of how things get handed down generationally. My father, a "surprise" baby who was born during the height of the Depression to a rather stone-cold mother, spent his life seeking validation from people and places that did nothing to build him up. As a result, he was unable to give or to receive love well. I said of him during his eulogy, that my dad was loveable, just not love-able. Despite his issues, he was a good man, harmless, and he and my mom found enough to reunite them later in life after connecting again at my wedding. Soon after that, they remarried.

Life is funny, isn't it?

I say all of this because I am challenged daily, in the midst of my own struggle, to acknowledge the need to "look under the bed." There are so many things that cause people to lash out, to make rash decisions, to run away as if their hair is on fire, because of fear—not of the wicked witch, but of what lurks within that has never had a light shined on it. People will burrow deep under the covers and think that doing so will protect them from some particular hurt ever finding them again.

It still does, though. It always does.

That is the paradox of pain. It is thought that if we keep our fears and hurts buried, rather than airing them out and dealing with them, we won't be harmed. The opposite, however, is true. Unresolved pain only grows bigger as we do. It never leaves the dark and dusty place beneath our mattress. It torments us until we jump up, brave in our quest to confront it, and examine what it truly looks like. It is only then that we can size it up and put it into perspective. When we confront our fears head on, we initiate true healing.

I heard someone say once that "pain buried alive never dies." I believe this.

It is also said that "hurt people, hurt people." We will talk about this more in another chapter. For now, I will simply say that there is always more to the story. There is always a reason deep within each of us that causes us to see the world, and each other, as we do. Our fears, if we allow them to, have power. They cause us to act irrationally at times. They spurn us on, and we succumb to fight or flight.

They ruin relationships.

They become more entrenched with age.

They lurk under the surface long past the time we are grown and should know better. In fact, we don't even realize that there is a connection to what our circumstances are and the buried fears that trigger them.

Thankfully, God knows all about this. It is part of the reason He sent His Son to be the Light of the World. It is when we give to Him all those scary, broken places within that we can be free from what they do to us.

My grace is sufficient for you, for my power is made perfect in weakness. (2 Cor. 12:9)

Do you remember the dentist in the classic, animated *Rudolph the Red-Nosed Reindeer* story who pulls out the teeth of the scary snow monster on the Island of Misfit Toys? Think about your fears. When we allow God to go before us, he wrecks the plan of the enemy. Rather than living in fear, we can have confidence that God is our protector. Satan becomes a toothless foe. He loses his bite.

Instead of running away, we can run to our Father. He shields us and does the fighting for us! We are safe in His care.

No weapon formed against you will prevail, and you will refute every tongue that accuses you. This is the heritage of the servants of the Lord, and this is their vindication from me. (Isa. 54:17)

I believe that fear and unresolved pain go hand in hand. We spend so much energy protecting ourselves from things that happened long ago. We are subconsciously obsessed with building up walls so that what hurt us doesn't happen again. We lose sight of the fact that, in our avoidance, we create more problems.

A child who grows up not feeling wanted or loved will likely have difficulty in committed relationships. Depending emotionally on another person, or being able to effectively discern issues of conflict, brings up pain and insecurities from the past.

I used to say of my father that it was like loving someone through a plate glass window. I could see him, engage with him on some level; but to reach out and connect with his soul, or touch that place within that made him who he was, was a challenge. I can recall very few occasions when I captured anything more than a glimpse. It is a sad truth to admit that we all paid for the sins of his mother, my paternal grandmother. It robbed my dad of enjoying the full experience of being loved and loving in return. It robbed my mom, my brothers, and me, and our kids, of experiencing deep, intimate relationships with him.

I am not suggesting that your husband was not loved as a child. With all certainty, this was not the case in my husband's situation. What I can say, however, is that we all carry "stuff." Sometimes, it is the horrific wounds that come from abuse or neglect. Others are more subtle but no less traumatic.

As a child, when someone we should trust injures us, the result can cause deficits in how we interpret our worth, our beauty, and our value on every level. It could be as simple as a teacher who embarrasses a child in front of the class in the third grade. There is no shelf life on something like that. It can cause debilitating shame for the rest of a person's life.

There is a reason why people run away. In my experience, they are running from what is not healed within them. They are still hiding from the monster under the bed.

It doesn't matter what age we are. We are all just children deep down inside.

For me, having covered up the hurts that were handed down to me from my dad, I carried them right into my relationship with my husband. There were things that profoundly affected me, and I wanted to be certain that those dysfunctions would not occur within my own home and family.

As a result, I overcompensated. That's what fear does. I drew boundaries as though with barbed wire so that there would be no misinterpretation about what I deemed acceptable behavior. The control, the means through which I kept things emotionally in order, only spawned more offenses. My husband also brought to our marriage his own set of unhealed wounds. We both had our flash points, and they were often in conflict with each other.

What seemed like a minor issue, like a tiny pebble in your shoe, had not overall affected our marriage for nearly twenty-five years. But then, intolerance on both sides built up to the point it tore us down. Both of us were "right." Both of us were damaged in our unique ways. What should have been resolved with counseling, love, and empathy grew into resentment.

When the root of our fears and hurts are not exposed, as good counseling will help do, then you can be sure it will overtake us. We do things to keep it all in check. We numb ourselves. We push it down deep, thinking it will go away on its own. We divert attention to it through our work, alcohol, shopping, gambling, or other destructive behaviors and relationships that only become problems on their own. There are no lack of places or ways to hide.

When the hiding no longer works, we break down. We act out. We turn from each other and from God, no longer wanting to be obedient.

We sin.

And sometimes, we just leave.

God, however, will always find us. He will let us do our thing. He will allow us to have our tantrums and carry on as the grown-up versions of the little kid whose hurts need soothing. He will let us think that we are justified in the chaos and for our hurting others with our words and actions. We may even go on, showing ourselves to the world as fully capable of righting what we perceive as our wrongs.

By golly, no one is going to tell us what to do! We deserve to have a little fun after all that we have been through!

Then when we huff and puff enough, when we get good and full of ourselves and our sin, He will let us fall.

Jonah was a servant of the Lord who was very angry about the disobedience happening around him. He was fed up with life and fed up with all the evil and debauchery that had become so prevalent.

He wanted nothing to do with it, and rather than deal with it as the Lord's ambassador, he turned his back in disgust.

"Go to the great city of Nineveh and preach against it, because its wickedness has come up before me," God said.

Instead, Jonah fled. He hopped on a ship heading for Tarshish, thinking that he could escape God's command. Out at sea, God sent a violent storm. Jonah admitted to the crew that he was a Hebrew who worshiped the Lord, and they became frightened.

In order to quiet the wind, Jonah told them that they would need to throw him overboard so that they would not become victims of God's wrath. They did just what he said to do. They picked up Jonah and threw him into the raging sea. Immediately, the storm calmed, and Jonah was swallowed up by a whale.

This is what it feels like when we are running from our problems and from God. We run from one storm only to get swallowed up into the belly of another. We get isolated from dealing with what God would have us do, yet we are trapped in ways we can no way anticipate through the bondage of a different kind.

Luckily for Jonah, he knew to do what God asks of us all. From inside the fish, he prayed.

In my distress I called to the Lord, and he answered me. From the depths of the grave I called for help, and you listened to my cry. (Jon. 2:2)

What Jonah did, is what we all try from time to time. We think we can outsmart God. We think that we can stray from doing what is right, doing what He asks of us; and that somehow, we will get away with it. God lets us drift out into the abyss just so far. We take the bait of the enemy in any number of ways, and we think that the hook is in someone else's mouth and not our own.

God will let us run aground on our own steam, being led by an undercurrent of pride and ego, thinking we know what is best.

We all play Jonah. We all think we can outswim the whale. This is how we guarantee ourselves an all-expense paid trip to the Harbor of Humility.

Although it doesn't feel like it at the time, humility is our safe place. It is where God reaches us, listening for our cry for help. He takes us from our sin and spits us out new again. God asked him after he was safely on shore, delivered by Whale Express to where God had told Jonah to go in the first place, "Do you have a right to be angry?"

Jonah replied, "I do." He said, "I am angry enough to die."

How often does our hurt and anger cause us to do things that God would not have us do?

In dealing with your husband, has your anger ever fueled you to the point where you don't care who you hurt?

Have you been to Tarshish lately? I know I have.

We cannot anticipate the way that God will redirect us so that we get on the right ship.

All I know is that He will.

I believe that humility is God's method of choice. By way of some divinely plotted map, He will cause us to look hard at how far we have drifted off course, how far we have distanced ourselves from Him. In these moments, we often feel afraid, alone, and ashamed.

We yearn to come close again. We yearn for His forgiveness and grace. We want to know the quickest route back to who He intends for us to be and His plan for us.

Your husband may well be happy as a clam at low tide right now, but I assure you, God knows exactly where he is too. He's watching for the red flare that signals an opening for Him to do His work. You may or may not ever know when this happens, but I promise you, it will.

In the meantime, we must guard our hearts from spewing animosity and blame. If you've ever seen one of those "killer whale" shows at Sea World and have sat too close to the front, you know that what spouts from the great mammal's blow hole, or from his splashing in the tank, can cause you to get soaking wet. There is no avoiding it. Unless you're wearing a rain slick, you're in for it!

Be careful.

Our hurts and anger never just stay inside the tank.

When our kids witness this, the damage that is done can create a generational chain reaction.

I am living proof of it.

The world won't help you in your time of humility. In fact, it does all it can to shake you from it. It will call you outside, tempt you, put a drink in your hand with a fancy little umbrella and celebrate with you on your cruise to Tarshish.

It will speak to you about your destination and all that awaits you in your new port. There will be dancing and carrying on, the likes of which you could never have as a boring, covenant-keeping, married person.

Come on, Jonah! Live a little!

But it's when you are out there at night, the raging sea battering against the ship, that you finally admit it would be best if you were on your way to Nineveh. That's when you need to know that it's never too late to turn back.

God is waiting for you. Instead of a whale, He will walk on water to get you back to shore.

Humility will guide you like a lighthouse. It's a buoy in the storm. Although you usually find it once you have hit bottom, it's where reconciliation lives, with Him and with yourself. It's the place where your heart can be open to others you have hurt and who have hurt you.

You may be way off course, but He will always show you the way home. Just ask Him.

There was a book I used to read to my kids, "If You Give a Pig a Pancake." This book, by Laura Numeroff, tells the whimsical tale of all that will happen if a little girl decides to share a bite of her breakfast.

"If you give a pig a pancake, she'll want some syrup to go with it. You'll give her some of your favorite maple syrup. She'll probably get all sticky, so she'll want to take a bath."

It's a fun book to read, and it makes a great point. Everything we do creates a response that we can hardly imagine.

It may not have begun with a pancake, but something happened to you, to your husband, and it started a chain reaction a long time ago. What happened is not your fault, nor is it his. Somewhere along the way, a fear or behavior was instilled that has its root in a place that was never mended. These unhealed wounds create chaos.

Where there is chaos, there is hurt. And blame. And unforgiveness. Hurt people, hurt people. And hurt people, run.

That monster that lurks under your bed? Find out what it is. Size it up. Let God heal it. Have empathy enough to at least acknowledge that there is always more to the story. There are flying monkeys that lurk beneath your husband's mattress too.

Though it is never God's plan for us to run, he has arranged for us to meet Him when we land in a place we never intended so that He can point us in the right direction again.

I know how scary things can get. Resist the urge to hide, and instead allow the light of God to show you where your broken places lie. They are not just the ones that developed since your husband left. They go deeper. Just like your husband's do.

We often want only to fix what is the immediate problem. We want to point our fingers at what hurts now, at what was done to us. But if we look deeply, retrospectively, we can follow the breadcrumbs and find Hansel and Gretel when they were young and realize some things we didn't want to see before.

We don't know why Jonah had to go through all that running and trauma, only to end up where God intended him to begin with. I don't know why you must suffer the difficulties and pain that comes with the voyage you are now on either.

All I know is that healing will come when we look closely at the dark and dusty places within us. Everything connects somehow. *Everything.*

Humility is not a weakness, but a strength. Use this time to get in touch with all those hidden places and learn from them.

The Lord is coming to you on the water, and in His hands are healing and solace and forgiveness. He will take you to your new season, free from the witches and flying monkeys of your past. You will land in a safe place once again, just where God intends for you to be.

Keep your eyes on the horizon.

Better days are ahead!

For everyone who exalts himself will be humbled and he who humbles himself will be exalted. (Luke 14:11)

The days are filled with things to do—rooms to paint, purging, and reorganizing. I am fine. The moments still come, thinking of who he used to be and of who he has become. I shake my head. I try so hard to reconcile the two very different men. But I can't. I simply can't. And that, perhaps, will never end. From the author's journal

8

Out of Order

THINGS COME TO ME in strange ways. For some reason, the shower seems to be the place when a thought will run through my head like a rabbit being chased by a dog. That quick, it will fly by my consciousness and—if I don't grab hold of it—I fear it will be gone forever. When they come to me this way, I know that I am to pay attention.

These kinds of thoughts aren't like reminders of what I need to add to my grocery list. They are phrases that are dropped into my spirit. Either as an answer to a question or a revelation, they plop into my psyche, and I will mull over the context for days.

You won't perhaps find this statement so hugely original or relevant. But to me, when it came to me one morning from out of nowhere in particular, I stood looking wide-eyed through the steamy glass perimeter as if I had just been handed a telegram from God. *"Things that are out of order for so long seem normal, but they're not."*

Again, I know that doesn't sound like the crib-note explanation to the Theory of Relativity, but it rocked my world just a little bit.

We have spent a lot of time here discussing how our situations have caused us to become undone in many ways. We've gone through cycles of shock, depression, hysteria, humility; and somehow, we still miss the one who has subjected us to this.

As if deep down inside, we deserved it.

Several months into my separation, once again in the shower, another jackrabbit of a thought hopped into my head. It was a command, really, and one that I did not want to do. *Read your old journals. Read them.*

I had to stop, mid-shampoo, and tackle that one.

I was afraid. *What in the world would that help? Won't that only make me more upset, God?* I mean, my journals, simple 6 inches by 8 inches lined notebooks, are stashed all over my house—in drawers, on shelves, in my nightstand. They are the unabashed chronicles of a wife and mother. I penned so many thoughts, dashing them off in the middle of the night when I couldn't sleep, or in between waiting for a school bus and pasta to boil. They held my prayers, my dreams, my hurts, my wants.

They are undisciplined. They are raw. They are the herkie-jerky tales of a half-baked life. But they held something else too. And God, forever omniscient, felt it was high time I reopened them.

So I did.

It's painful when we look back, reliving the ups and downs. It's like watching a movie in reverse. We know how things worked out, or didn't. We see our whiny expectations, drawn like pictures across a page, that make us wince at our own shallowness, and others, where we take a gulp of pride and thank God for the redeeming insight that showed we had some depth and substance. You know the trends, seeing that God's hand was on your life, your kids, your forward progress. There are jewels that we uncover about our lives that, when we look back over the years, we are grateful for our tenacity, our courage, and our faith.

But like every other life, there are the not-so-stellar moments that are recorded with tongue-in-cheek euphemisms. Some are quite humorous. Some, just sad. Underneath it all, I saw the prequel to the crash that took the legs out from under me.

There is a saying that I've heard that goes like this: "What you tolerate, persists." This statement is so very true, isn't it?

Like the sassy toddler who is so cute, making you laugh under your breath at her determined finger, pointing out the reasons why she should be allowed to eat cookies for dinner and not green beans, it happens to us. We toggle with the margins of acceptability, wanting to give grace and deference just a little bit. We want to be loved and remembered for being fun, being able to excuse a little extra ice cream on top of the cone with a wink and a nod. That's the good stuff.

We forget though, that how even harmless things, left unchecked, can turn on its head and bite you back.

So it was with me.

Reading those journals came as a shock. There were bits and pieces of seemingly minor episodes that splashed colorfully across the messy handwritten pages; but when added together, piled one on top of the other, they painted a picture of a marriage that had become imbalanced.

When one of us is struggling, it's natural for the other to pick up the slack. We assume more of the responsibilities. We hoist the burdens of a growing, busy family on our shoulders and carry on.

My husband worked extremely hard, and though I also held a job, finances were a challenge for lots of reasons. With all his efforts and taking side work when he could, I gladly took on wearing more of the hats so that he would not be bothered by the normal day-to-day life headaches. I thought I was doing the right thing.

The problem is the more I did, the less he had to do; and the less he did, the greater the ability to disengage in other ways naturally followed. My actions disempowered him. In my mind, I was helping. In his mind, he began to feel that he was needed only to provide for the general welfare of our family, meaning financially. Everything else, emotionally, spiritually, or physically, I had it covered.

As they say, it's hard to know what comes first, the chicken or the egg. So much of life becomes a vicious cycle without our even knowing it. We do one thing, not expecting to affect another, but it's all related.

The less my husband did, the more he resisted wanting to, and the greater the intimacy of our marriage partnership suffered. It's that old "killing them with kindness" thing. In short, my husband grew in his unhappiness, and I grew in my frustration at his disinterest and detachment.

When the car is skidding off the road, it's too late to make sure your seatbelt is on. You can sense the collision coming and brace for it, but all you can do is slam on the brakes and pray you don't hit anything. The impact is always more shocking than you can comprehend at the time.

So much of the damage was already done.

We began fighting. Making up. Fighting again. We would have long talks, agreements of understanding, a weekend here and there of rekindling, a few bouts of counseling. We were falling and scraping our knees and bandaging ourselves up so often, we never fully healed from one episode before another would strike.

Still, we didn't want to admit that things were *that* bad. At least I didn't.

There is a place we come to where we can never imagine the audacity of words we say, or hear said, to us. These are the words *other* married people say who don't love each other. They are clichéd, movie-script phrases that you hear often in chick flicks.

"I need a break from you." "I'm just done." "You don't ever help me." "How could you?" "So what you are saying is that you want to try life without me?"

I recall thinking, when these statements got bantered about, that they were more for shock value to sober us up. I expected that they would cause us to sit up straighter, look at each other tearfully in the eyes, and promise that we would never say them again.

Funny thing about that is:

The tongue has the power of life and death; and those who love it will eat its fruit. (Prov. 18:21)

Rather than the paddles shocking our unsteady hearts back into rhythm, we were polarized even more.

Fights lasted, not minutes or hours, but days, and then weeks.

Tearful making up and professions of love patched us up for a bit. Until the next train screamed down the track, ready to derail.

Other things happened. Friendships. Text messages. Secrets. Behaviors that are not conducive to faithful love and matrimony. That proverbial grass on the other side of the fence got greener and greener by the day.

Angry rants.

Bad language.

Accusations that flew like rockets.

The summer of discontent added other "dis-" words: discouragement, disengaged, disrespect. I wrote about it in my pages like footnotes and afterthoughts framed in prayers that God would heal all.

Oh, if only I could go back and rewrite the script.

What happens when God sees what is before us but we are too blurry-eyed in denial to know what to expect? He places a hedge of protection around us that doesn't soften the blow but sustains us in it. Sort of like feathering a nest for us, knowing that we will soon be in it, and alone.

God feels distant, but He is not. He knows that we are reeling, spinning out of control.

He waits.

He knows that it won't be long, and we will be calling out to Him. But first, we are going to do all we can on our own steam. We are going to try our hand at doing the very same things that got us into this mess.

With the same effort we threw into picking up the slack, we throw ourselves into fixing things.

We attempt every conceivable means to get our husband's attention. We go into overdrive, proving to him that we are simply not going to give up and throw in the towel. That's not who we are. We go about showing him that we are going to change. As frosting on the cake, we silently resolve to change *him*.

We vow that everything is going to be good again!

To prove our points, we accept the blame, hoist up our big-girl panties, and go about keeping all those plates spinning, just like they used to do on the *Ed Sullivan Show*. We run back and forth, full of hyper-energy. We are masters of our own universe. Everything is humming along nicely.

It's so ingrained in us. We live as though on a seesaw, working hard to make sure life stays balanced. We make certain that everyone has what they need, that no one feels left out. Where the weight is so not evenly distributed, we push and pull to re-center the fulcrum.

We are superwoman after all!

We get so busy, trying to bolster up what is sagging, that we don't realize until we turn around and discover it.

He is gone.

All those plates come suddenly crashing down around you, and it bites. What is out of order for so long seems normal, but it's not.

Just so you don't feel thrown under the bus, know that this is an equal opportunity catastrophe.

In our earnestness to do for our spouses, one must extend, or assume, the offer to help. But so must the other person allow that help to persist. This is critical.

As hard as it is to understand, God didn't design it that way. He created us from man's rib. We are supposed to be at his side, not towering over him, or not doing for him what he should, by nature, do for us. God intended for us to be cherished and loved, honored and respected by our men. Our husbands are to be our covering, protecting us, praying over and with us.

And God expects that we do the same for our husbands, not in a superior way, but in a compatible, righteous way.

We simply were not created to do it all, no matter what the world tells us.

I think, honestly, that I misinterpreted Proverbs 31 for years. That woman, you know the one that "sets about her work vigorously, her arms are strong for her tasks." I desired to be the "wife of noble character." I wanted to use my gifts to help my husband so that he would find my worth "far more valuable than rubies." It was my intention for his gifts to shine and for mine to complement. It just didn't get perceived that way.

Anxiety and adrenalin, compounded by the extra coffee we must consume in order to stay awake and focused, cause us to operate as if electro-kinetically. Our hair, our being, every touch we make seems to "zap" in response to all the nervous energy running through our bodies.

So it is when our marriages break. Like a tornado, we take a swath of anything in our path that might prevent our efforts to mend it. It's as if we believe it is our sole duty and responsibility to make things right again.

We insist that our husbands listen to us, that they come back and respond to our need for them. They must be made aware of the grave consequences that their decision to leave us brings. We are compelled with the need to explain ourselves, certain that for all these years, they had us wrong.

After he left, I tried so many ways to reach my husband. It didn't matter how subtle my intentions were; he stonewalled me. He was the one who left, yet I was the one trying desperately to find a way so that he would let me in. Out of fear, my compulsion to reason with him only drove the wedge further between us.

My once warm, kindhearted husband, turned ice cold. He became a stranger.

And I became just like Balak.

Do you remember him? He was the son of Zippor, king of Moab, who was filled with fear of the Israelites who were camped out along the Jordan and poised to overtake the land. He called upon the prophet, Balaam, to come to Moab so he could use his anointing with the Lord to remedy a solution. Balak even offered to pay Balaam, God's messenger, handsomely for the deed. In short, he wanted to convince Balaam to curse the Israelites and render them incapable of doing harm to Moab. However, the prophet was only able to speak what the Lord would give to him to deliver.

In Balak's mind, his plan was sound. The influence he was trying to ensure was only to protect his kingdom. His motives, he thought, were pure. He believed in God. He believed that if he could just cause Balaam the Prophet to understand his concern, that he would put in a good word for him, and the Lord would grant his request. Balak wanted to influence the outcome in the way that *he* thought things should go.

Three times, Balak took Balaam to different spots to survey the Israelites and the potential they posed to encroach on his kingdom. At each site, Balak would build seven altars and offer a sacrifice so that Balaam could inquire favorably with God as to what he would say.

Instead of cursing the Israelites, however, God's response was to bless them. This was the exact opposite of Balak's intentions! Each time Balaam spoke of what the Lord gave him, Balak would insist he inquire again. But with each intercession, the results only increased the blessing of the Israelites. For added insult, Balaam was told by the Lord to share that the kingdom of Moab would come to ruin. Finally, in frustration, Balak's anger burned against the prophet.

Balaam, however, insisted, "I could not do anything of my own accord, good or bad, to go beyond the command of the Lord."

It's not that the Israelites were a perfect people. They weren't. In fact, the very next chapter, Numbers 25, speaks of the sexual immorality of the men as well as the idol worship of Baal. They had begun as well to intermarry the Moabite women. All of these were sins, and God would have His way to deal with them.

I don't know exactly why this passage came so heavily to my spirit. It seems in our desperation to be heard, to fix what burdens us, to frantically connect on some level with our husbands so that we can feel whole again, we stop trusting God to do it His way.

Like Balak, we insist that God is not answering us, as if maybe He does not fully understand our situation. We reason that we are only trying to help Him a little, as if He needs a nudge in the right direction.

We build an altar, like we might cook our husband his favorite meal to entice him back into our kitchen, only to have it grow cold on the stove. We sit alone in the candlelight, dejected and gutted by the new reality that we no longer have influence at all over what he does or does not do.

It's hard as women, especially when we are so used to doing so much to control and contribute to our family dynamics, that we take our hands *completely* off the wheel and let God drive.

That is, honestly, what I believe we are to do.

How else can God deal with our husbands? It needs to be His voice he hears in his heart and spirit, not ours. Besides, if he is like mine, your husband is likely in a place where what you say will not be listened to. Silence speaks louder than words. Trust me.

When we get ahead of God, we are out of order.

God knows how to reach your husband. He doesn't need help from his best friend, or his brother, the one who feels like you do, that he is making a mistake. He doesn't need the pastor, whose sermon seems to have been written just for him and that you texted to him the link to listen to.

If a man has skidded off the road to righteousness, only God can bring him back. Yes, He can work through others to do so, but let Him orchestrate that, not you.

So what do you do? You measure yourself. You respond appropriately as a woman of grace and with the strength of knowing He will do what He will do. That He will fight on your behalf and, no matter where your husband has gone to escape, He can reach him and convict his heart.

The question is not *if* He will do it. He will. It's just whether your husband pays heed—and that is between him and God. If he does, there is nothing that will keep your husband from doing what God, and his conscience, tell him to. But if he does not, if in his free will he chooses not to—either for a season or forever—the outcome that God has for you will not be made different.

What this means is that God has you no matter what it looks or feels like right now.

No one wants to be forced to do something. Even in his sin, your husband must be led by his own heart. If it is made of stone or made of flesh, it will beat on its own. You wouldn't want him back any other way.

What we tolerate, persists.

I know that this is counterintuitive, but I believe that the less said, the better. It is best that we conduct ourselves as rationally, openly, and graciously as possible. I understand fully how challenging this is especially in the face of such hurt and wounding.

On a practical level, this may mean contacting him only when absolutely necessary, sticking to the matter at hand and not giving in to the impulse to react or show our own torrid emotions. Again, easier said than done; but with prayer, practice, and the understanding that you are stepping out of the way so that God can step in is huge.

Anything we do to monopolize the emotional spectrum, to inflict guilt or shame, to give him any reason to react negatively, will only end up making things worse and hurting you more. I have made every mistake known in this area. Please understand that I am speaking from my experience to save you being schooled in this lesson. When, and if, your husband softens to the possibility of being reached or reaching out to you, it will come via you holding your head high and your tongue still.

Difficult as it is, God will honor your obedience.

It will seem at times that your husband has all the influence. That what his new life has become away from you is some sort of nirvana. Remember, that if he is outside the will of God, it is only a mirage. Trust God that He knows all.

You must do only what He gives you to do, and that is to be still. Pray. Seek Him. Do not take matters into your own hands.

"I could not do anything of my own accord, good or bad, to go beyond the command of the Lord."

When Balak sent for Balaam, he had an expectation that he was in control and that he would gain the upper hand over the Israelites. He would have been better off had he never assumed such a willful act. So will it be for you as well.

Don't get ahead of God. Find solace in knowing that His order for our lives is for our own good. Anything outside of it is not normal.

Keep your seat belt on, and let God drive. Watch for the blessings to come.

> *And after you have done everything, stand. (Eph. 6:13)*

> *Blessed are those who hunger and thirst for righteousness for they will be filled. (Matt. 5:6)*

> *That is why, for Christ's sake, I delight in weakness, in insults, in hardships, in persecutions, in difficulties. For when I am weak, then I am strong. (2 Cor. 12:10)*

9

Love Anyway

GROWING UP, I WAS a huge Sonny and Cher fan. Their TV show had just started airing, and I was hooked, eagerly anticipating each weekly broadcast. I loved their music certainly, having, at one point, every record album and eight-track tape they ever made. But it wasn't that they were musically fantastic. It was their charisma, their cute bantering back and forth, the hip, passionate way they made fun of each other, the way Cher flipped her hair off her shoulder just before she landed a zinger. They could laugh, put each other down, and in the end sing "I Got You Babe" and everything was good.

That all struck a chord with a young girl whose life didn't seem so tidy. Sonny and Cher could tease and act offended, but you always got the sense that they loved each other anyway.

Simple as that sounds, it made an impression on me.

You don't need to be a trivia buff to know what happened next. A few years later, the tabloids that I so avidly perused on Saturday mornings at Vons Market while my mom shopped, delivered the blow. The beat of the Bonos was coming to an end. Though I shared the idyllic fantasy with a ton of other fans, sadly, even love wouldn't keep them together.

In real life, my parents divorced when I was six or seven. As such transitions are difficult for adults, they were as well for my brothers and me. My parents were good people. My mom had a knack for doing with little but making it seem like a lot. She made sure we went to church. She expected us to be honest and to do our best. My dad, a young bank executive, was more comfortable in his job, than his family. He was mostly absent by design for reasons I previously shared. Add to this the burden of alcoholism, and you can see that dysfunction reigned.

During these prepubescent years, and being the only girl, my mom thought it best to send me three thousand miles, from Los Angeles to Connecticut, the day after school got out in June until Labor Day, the day before school started again. By this point, she was a single mom, back into the work force as a bank teller and trying to keep everyone safe and accounted for. My grandparents were the logical guardians for me. It was not a punishment. I loved being with them! During those summers, I was an only child with doting, loving caregivers.

They lived in a small factory town, on a three-acre property surrounded by woods and those New England stone walls that made one think of a Robert Frost poem. It was on a long-paved drive way that I road my Western Flyer bike, imagined plenty of adventures, and watched the tall oak trees move with the breeze and drop their acorns as if they were greeting me and could sense the questions that were always rattling around in my head.

To me, my grandparents were, by all rights rock stars too. They were gracious, hardworking people. They loved to entertain and had many friends. When they retired, they opened up the only laundromat in town, which they kept warm and clean. When they would go there to check on it, people greeted them as if they were royalty. I observed so many, many times my grandmother cupping the chin of a child and saying, "Hello there, honey." My grandfather, reaching out his hand to someone as if they stood in his living room, not his place of business.

I learned so very much during these summers. By their example, my grandparents taught me how to treat others with dignity and respect.

They taught me how to work hard. They taught me the meaning of character and integrity. They taught me not to be afraid of thunderstorms. They threw for me my very first birthday party, and though I didn't know any kids in town, they found a few and invited them to be my friends.

They taught me how to mow the lawn. They taught me how to fix things. They taught me how to plant flowers and take out old rotting tree stumps. And when people disappoint us, they taught me how to love them anyway.

When September would come, and the first hint of fall touched the tips of the trees in the woods, I became sullen and quiet. How I didn't want to leave them and the special bond we had.

Back in the suburbs of Los Angeles, my mom was doing all she could, minding my brothers and keeping food on the table. My dad was nowhere around. My second oldest brother, just twelve or thirteen at the time, started hanging out at the home of a friend who lived with his uncle and did all the things boys like to do, like hunt and fish. Before long, the uncle decided that Montana would be the perfect place to live and raise two boys, and in the dead of night, packed up and left without a trace. It's a story that, to this day, I am unable to fill in the blanks as to what happened to the brother that I loved. I can say only that the hole he left was deep and wide. I watched my mom age, helpless in her mission to find him. Years later, during the summer after I graduated high school, a miracle happened and God healed that wound. My brother, though he still lives in Montana, came back to us.

The twelve years he was away, we never stopped praying for him. My mom did everything she could to find him through private investigators and legal means. My grandmother prayed novenas and kept the flame of hope alive, but it was hard. Brainwashed, my brother had been told that his family didn't care about him and that attempts to reach us or acknowledge us would do him harm. But we loved him anyway.

I only had my grandfather for a few more summers before he died. He was strong and righteous. He was honest and well respected. He didn't have to say much to say a lot. He died in October the year I was ten. Though my mom was the only one who traveled for the funeral, she reported to us when she came home that there wasn't an empty chair at his wake. Half the town, it seems, came to pay their respects.

My grandfather didn't want to leave us, but he had to. We loved him anyway.

I watched my grandmother closely, still living with her each summer. She missed him terribly, but stood for him, carrying on with the businesses they had built together, maintaining their home and property and friendships. She was a remarkable, wonderful woman who impacted my life in countless ways. Had my mom not thought to send me to them from that first summer, I honestly do not know who I would have become. There was so much in my life that could have put me on a very different path. I thank God for this gift.

Years later, Gram would care for my first two children from infancy while my husband and I worked. The love that she had for them and the joy that we all shared together are among my greatest and most treasured memories.

From early on, life was always in a state of needing to pick up the pieces and start again. My most stable years, truly, were the first twenty-five of the twenty-nine that I was married. Which may explain why this transition has been so very difficult for me personally.

As most lessons are, it is not until you can step back from the place you are in, with some time and perspective, and find the jewels among the thorns. We all have a story. Our journeys are littered with fallen icons and people who have, deliberately or unintentionally, done harm to us. There is no way to go through life without events that are earmarked as milestones. Victories or tragedies, we all know them.

Regardless of how hard we try, how kind we are, how much we stand for what is right, there are going to be things that happen to us. There is a definite ebb and flow of life. People will love us unconditionally, being there for us through thick and thin, and others will walk away. And, in different degrees, we will do the same.

I am learning that sin and righteousness coexist in this world. Just like good and evil. There can be, within the same breath, love and hate. It's wearisome to think how easily we give in to one at the expense of the other.

The Tree of Knowledge was in the Garden of Eden from the beginning. In fact, it is said that it was located smack dab in the middle of it. Just how long Adam and Eve dwelled there before Eve was tempted to take that fateful bite of the apple, we don't know. But that's how it works, I think. You don't start in life with the intention of doing bad, of becoming defiant, of sinning. We don't expect to have difficulties, just like we don't get married while also believing that we will get divorced. It all happens, bit by bit. We drift just enough to justify being off course, and then the serpent finds his opening.

Temptation always exists, surrounding us, beckoning our senses to gaze upon forbidden fruit. It all depends on what we allow in, who we listen to, how easily we let the tempter sit upon our shoulder and whisper to us about the attraction of sin.

Stolen water is sweet; food eaten in secret is delicious! (Prov. 9:17)

That is why God wants us to stay close to Him, to remain obedient to his commands. Good things and bad things happen to everyone. We all want trouble to stay far from us, but sometimes, it finds us, and we must endure it. By abiding in the Lord, wherever our journey takes us, He will cover us, protect us, and give us strength. He will show us the way home.

He who pursues righteousness and love, finds life, prosperity and honor. (Prov. 21:21)

It may not happen just the way we want it or when our expectations think it should. Hurts and difficulties last longer than we would like. We know that God never promised that our lives would be free from adversity. I'm sure even in the Garden of Eden, there were days when Adam and Eve tripped over a vine, slipped on a rock while gazing at a waterfall, or got bit by a snapping turtle. He just warns us to stay clear of the things that injure our soul, our spirit, and our relationship with Him and with each other.

In addition to His Word, God gives us wisdom, bidding us to follow it. The Holy Spirit that lives within us speaks to our consciences, to our desires to live in His will and to enjoy the fruits of His plans for us.

The foolish, however, have a much different fate. Conforming to the world leads to emptiness, betrayal, and sin. As if they think that their ways will be undetected, they turn off their internal GPS, that which God gives us to know right from wrong, and travel at warp speed without a compass. Where they land will always be far different from where they started, and never in the place they thought they were heading.

Like me, you are likely still in a season of picking up the pieces and trying to start again. It's important that you understand that what happened is not a result of you not being good enough. God would never have caused what has happened with your husband. There is nothing that you could have said or done differently that ultimately would have changed the present outcome. In word or deed, the temptation to leave the garden was there, coexisting with the covenant to stay. Whatever the serpent's method was that called to your husband like a pied piper, he left because sin won out. That's on him. Period.

Now comes the ultimate question: Can you love him anyway?

Sometimes, loving someone means letting them go. It means surrendering to the fight that you can change what has happened. It's a stage of acceptance that takes us a while to get to and does not come without hurt.

Sometimes, the worst thing that can happen to us ends up bringing us to the best. And sometimes, what we think would be the best thing that could happen ends up bringing us to the worst.

There is a peace that comes over us when we give up the fight. We know that we gave it our all. We can know that we did not walk quietly into that dark night, but did so with our heads high and our hearts full. It doesn't mean for certain that all hope is lost. It just means, as we have shared together over the course of this book, that if God performs the miracle of resurrection on our marriages, it is as all things are, up to Him to do it. And, if it's not in His plans to do so, then we must trust that He has better for us.

There are things that only God can teach your husband as he stands before Him in the wilderness, covered only by a fig leaf, and there are things that you will learn too. It starts with trusting Him that He will not leave you exiled, wandering aimlessly. He absolutely has a plan.

Now to him who is able to do immeasurably
more than all we ask or imagine, according to his
power that is at work within us. (Eph. 3:20)

I know how our minds work. There are caveats, right? There are situations that if I knew about, hidden deep within your marital closet, I would release you from the question of doing what may be hard to do. After all, the battles you are facing, the destruction of your marriage, has come at tremendous cost. There must be exceptions, special considerations, admonitions, that would usurp this golden rule and make it void.

But there aren't.

Above all else, love each other. (1 Pet. 4:8)

No matter how he treats you. No matter what he's done. No matter how unwilling he is to acknowledge you, validate you or own up to how he has hurt you.

Don't misunderstand. I am in no way saying that you just stand there and take whatever is dished out. There must be boundaries that are drawn, rules of engagement that provide for your safety and your sanity when interaction or communication is required, and your present relationship is tenuous and difficult. I suggest strongly that you seek guidance from a good counselor as well as seek the resource of many good books on the subject of boundaries.

Loving someone who has hurt you so deeply isn't easy, but not loving someone you were bound to in covenant is harder. Whatever happened within your husband is evidence of a struggle, that again, has little to do with you. You are merely the excuse, not the cause, no matter what he says to the contrary.

When King Saul, in jealousy, crisscrossed the countryside in pursuit of David, David would cause no harm to come to him. Saul was out to kill David. At least twice, David had him in his sight, yet he had mercy and spared his life. After years of being on the run, when it was reported to him that Saul was dead, David wept for the Lord's anointed.

He loved him anyway.

When the prodigal son demanded his half of his inheritance so that he could go off and pursue wild living and spend his treasure on all sorts of debauchery, his father was deeply hurt. It would seem likely that his father may also have suffered mockery and humiliation from his kinfolk and elders about the foolishness of his decision to let the boy do what he did. But his father's hope was in the Lord. Without any way of knowing the fate his son would meet, he chose to believe in the son that he had raised, not in the one he had become. He prayed for his son. He focused not on the hurt, but on the hillside where he would one day see him returning in the distance.

He loved him anyway.

Joseph's brothers, after conspiring to kill him, threw him into a pit and later sold him to a caravan of Ishmaelites. After years and many trials, when his brothers were before him, humbled and hungry, unaware that they were bowing before their long-lost brother who was now in charge of all the land in Egypt, Joseph had pity and mercy upon them. He restored them in relationship and in provision, and bestowed on them the forgiveness of his heart.

He loved them anyway.

You intended to harm me, but God intended it for good. (Gen. 50:20)

We don't understand the trials we must endure. We just know that we will endure them. God will equip us, reinforcing our foundation of faith so that we are sustained. He gives us glimpses of hope that good will prevail. When we mess up, when we sin, when we act in ways that we need to repent for, He watches us from above and gives us grace.

He loves us anyway.

We can do the same. Loving our husbands does not mean they deserve it. It does not exonerate them for the harm they have done. It does not say it's okay that they have hurt you. It simply says that their turmoil belongs to them, and you have chosen to believe God for what comes next.

God wants us to keep going, to keep striving. He wants us to love anyway.

The prodigal son came home. David was made king. Joseph saved countless lives from famine after he endured the pit and prison.

My brother, though he was kidnapped and yanked from our family, is a good, wonderful man with a huge heart and a beautiful family of his own. My parents, after twenty years, reunited and my dad learned to celebrate his family. Even Cher, at Sonny's funeral, wept as she acknowledged that there would not have been stardom without the love of a short, mustached man who had taken a skinny, teen-aged girl with a big voice under his wing.

Things have a way of coming full circle. God is always in the storm. He always makes things right no matter how bad it seems.

The beat, always will, go on.

Love anyway.

10

The Harvest

I WAS A YOUNG GIRL when the movie *Love Story* came out. For those of you who were not even a twinkle yet in the 1970s, let me tell you, you missed out on a classic. It was the very first movie, besides *Old Yeller*, and maybe *Bambi*, that I can remember crying. It starred Ryan O'Neal and Ali MacGraw, and was based on a novel by Erich Segal. The plot was about Oliver Barrett IV, a Harvard Law School student from a wealthy family, and Jenny, whose roots were the typical working-class-wrong-side-of-the-track lineage. Of course, Oliver and Jenny fall madly in love and get married. When, in protest, Oliver's father cuts them off financially, they endure making ends meet the old-fashioned way, Oliver as a lawyer and Jenny as a teacher. Life is wonderful until it is discovered that Jenny has leukemia, and the struggle becomes real. The movie succeeds in all the right ways at pulling the heartstrings.

Even if you are not familiar with the movie title, at some time or another, you have likely heard this famous quote, "Love means never having to say you're sorry." It's a line that seems profound, deep, and affecting. In the movie, it works.

But in real life, it's hard to find a scenario to which it would be appropriate. I mean, shouldn't we always say we're sorry? When we love someone, shouldn't we be *even more* inclined to apologize and make certain we are reconciled with each other?

Ah, if only real life were so simple. Life can feel so surreal sometimes, doesn't it? We are thrust into the uncomfortable place of trying to figure all this out as we go.

Our situations are layered with hurt feelings, separation, property issues, allowances, and all kinds of division to mitigate. The whole stratosphere that comes with "uncoupling" is not exactly the breeding ground for peace and tranquility. Especially when one party is an unwilling participant.

Who can even think about apologies?

For me, it feels a bit like *my* life is a movie. One moment, I am the heroine, like Scarlet O'Hara, clutching the earth of Tara and swearing, "As God is my witness, I shall never be hungry (angry/betrayed/unloved) again!" In another, I am sullen, adopting a pseudo-anonymity like a double agent, communicating in code or invisible ink so as not to be discovered for all my vulnerabilities and unhealed places.

In major scenes, I am this healthy, grown woman who has survived the derailing of my life plans, yet still standing in faith for what God has for me. In minor ones, I am in bed by nine, books, journals, crossword puzzles, and Sudoku sprawled out next to me, glaring and highlighting the empty space like a flashing neon sign: *Alone! Alone! Alone!*

If not a movie, perhaps my life would be the plot of a boring—very boring—reality show.

So much in our situations is fluid. We are bombarded, words flung in attack or accusation, loose ends and compromise, all in an effort to land somewhere that feels even remotely normal. Each side is trying to gain an advantage, trying to prove a point. We are crazed with anxiety, blame, and circumstance, none of which resembles the life we knew. We are frazzled and petulant, constantly in some various phase of fight or flight.

If this is not enough, the world weighs in to tell us how we should be "over it" by now and should be making new "friends." With a wave of their hand, well-meaning folks offer, in a guise of encouragement, that we should try shedding our married look for something perhaps a little more hip and sexy.

Only we don't feel hip, and we certainly don't feel sexy.

Whatever it was supposed to mean in the movie, our love story ended with the line, "Love means never *hearing* the words 'I'm sorry,'" along with the addendum, "So don't expect it, wish it, or pray for it. It ain't coming. So there!"

Thankfully, God is not so pompous. He exchanges the judgement of others for His unconditional acceptance.

> *You, Lord, are forgiving and good, abounding*
> *in love to all who call on you. (Ps. 86:5)*

Things with God are pretty simple, actually. He wants us to love each other, to treat others the way we would want to be treated, and to offer an olive branch—and an open door—when things don't go so great. In other words, He knows we are going to mess things up from time to time, so He gives us some easy guidelines to follow, and nudges by the Holy Spirit, to help us keep it between the lines.

Even then, we still manage to channel our inner Rhett Butler when we should be offering grace: "Frankly, my dear, I don't give a damn."

The Bible tells us that we need to be reconciled for our differences. It doesn't care who is right or wrong, who started it, who is at fault, or the last thing someone said before hanging up the phone. It only tells us to mend our grievances and to be at peace with one another.

This is paramount to God.

> *And when you stand praying, if you hold any-*
> *thing against anyone, forgive them, so that your*

Father in heaven may forgive you your sins. (Mark 11:25)

The subject of making amends is straightforward. What about when we are not given the opportunity to do so? What about when one of you wants nothing to do with building a bridge? Or when our apologies aren't accepted? How many times do we have to accept responsibility for wrongs we did not commit just to bring peace? Or when the hurt is still just too fresh to think beyond the next five minutes?

Our grievances run deep and have names like Betrayal, Abandonment, and Unfaithfulness. Yet we are supposed to forgive?

Peter had a similar question for Jesus.

> *"Lord, how many times shall I forgive my brother or sister? Up to seven times?" Jesus answered, "I tell you, not seven times, but seventy-seven times." (Matt. 18:21–22)*

I know that there is always a "but," so let me help you out here:
Does God know what he did to me?
He does.
Does God know how hard I tried to make it work?
Yes, He knows.
Does God know that I didn't want him to leave? Or how much damage this has caused our kids? Our family?
He knew it then, and He knows it now. It hurts Him too.
God doesn't expect us to forgive all that has happened to us—at least not yet—when things are still so painful, does He?
He does.
Even when we aren't ready, even when we don't feel like it:

> *Bear with each other and forgive one another*
> *If any of you has a grievance against someone.*
> *Forgive as the Lord forgave you. (Col. 3:13)*

Repentance, reconciliation, and peace are always God's goal.

When we were kids, if our parents witnessed or heard about our hurting another person's feelings, we were told right there on the spot to "Say you're sorry."

I remember the physical obedience of doing so. For example, when my little brother took something that belonged to me and I retaliated, hurting him somehow in the process. I was marched immediately to stand in front of our kitchen refrigerator, told to confess what I had done, and utter the words of apology.

I can't say that I *felt* sorry in the moment, but I did it anyway.

I likely had a few good reasons in my head as to why, what I said or did, was justified due to the offense of taking what was mine.

No matter how weak or insincere my words were, they stuck. They soothed the hurt, caused my brother to stop crying, and reset the atmosphere. In the small transaction of apology and acceptance, my brother and I mended our breach and I became a little more sensitive to his feelings.

I apologized because I *had* to. Nevertheless, I learned a lesson, and it was a good one.

It seems that when we grow older, we take on a different approach to life. We are supposed to know better. We should have mastered those two little words that proved once to be so powerful. One would think that "I'm sorry" would become rote to us. As adults, we should have this whole thing down. We hurt someone's feelings, or they hurt ours, and apologies should be automatic.

However, the world is good at teaching us other lessons. It lists for us all the reasons why getting even is necessary, even profitable. We are told, "What goes around, comes around." Somehow, we need to be assured of the satisfaction of seeing to it that we make another pay for the harm they caused us. Revenge takes on a life of its own. There's a score to keep and we are like Rambo with a manicure.

But this is not God's way.

Do not gloat when your enemy falls; When he stumbles, do not let your heart rejoice. (Prov. 24:17)

I get how very difficult it is to simply stand, thinking we can do and say everything righteously. We are bound to mess up. We are humans after all. We rage and cry, and let fear drive us to some very dark places. We *want* to trust God. We want to believe for the best, holding on to the knowing that He is working all things out for our good.

Like being doused by a bucket of cold water, we are forced to look at our circumstances with an eye that is good for only what we can see or imagine in front of us. We know we are to walk by faith and not by sight, but what we see is scary and unnerving.

So we hold on to what has been trespassed against us. We linger at the party of pity just a bit longer than we should. We call him—the one who left—to get a rise, to level some guilt, to plead our case.

However, nothing makes a difference; so we get bitter, not better.

Once again, there is an opening for the enemy to stake a claim and convince us that we have a right to be angry. More than this, he tells us there is no hope for anything other than the hell we are going through now. We need to fight for what is right and let our husband know he just can't get away with what he's done, by golly! Moreover, for good measure, the devil throws in an old military analogy about the best defense being a good offense, or something like that.

Everything is cooked up like a secret potion or a poisoned apple to whet our whistle and get us to take a bite.

If I were standing in the garden with you, I would tell you what I, and countless others, have learned the hard way. "Run! It's a trap!"

Bitterness and unforgiveness, or said another way, an unwillingness to even *consider* that you can one day forgive your husband for his transgressions, will cause you only more heartache. I promise you.

God's plan for us is revealed in our seasons. Some are hard; others are plentiful. We work, serve, and sacrifice, all leading us to a place where we are supposed to understand the meaning of it all. It is in our obedience, in doing what God has for us to do, that we can anticipate a harvest rich in His blessings.

Even when nothing makes sense to us in the moment, it is best to always do what God would have us do.

Sometimes, God has his own version of plot twists that throw us for a loop. These seasons, like the one you are in now, all serve a purpose that will change us for the better if we allow God, and not our feelings of retribution, to lead us through it.

We reap what we sow. When we sow in faith, we trust His outcomes for our lives. What is sowed in love is not always returned in kind, but we are to not grow weary in doing so. God will honor our faithfulness, and our harvest will be blessed because of it.

It works in reverse too.

What happens when we sow bitterness? The product is hurt, blame, and vengeance. These are the harvest of shame, guilt, and pride; and they play right into a promised outcome of more division, unrest, and harm that can last generations.

Like when we were kids, we aren't always ready to offer or receive an apology.

Our present circumstances may prevent us from saying the things we want or allow us to extend an olive branch. Sometimes people are not willing to meet us half way. Even if someone that hurt you never says the words, "I'm sorry," forgive them anyway. Your spirit will hear it. God will too.

Holding on to hurt, hurts *us* greater than it hurts the other person. Studies prove that unforgiveness brings our energy low, closes us off emotionally, inhibits healing, causes our bodies to secrete toxins and stress hormones, such as cortisol, which raises all kinds of havoc, including cancer, and even ages us.

It has been said that bitterness is like drinking poison and expecting the other person to die. Science, and God who created us, proves that the opposite is true.

We die. Bit by miserable bit.

If you don't want to forgive your husband for his peace and wellbeing, then do it for yours.

In every transaction, there are two sides. Though it may be difficult for you to imagine yourself apologizing in the face of what *he* has done, I promise you, there is always room to do so. No matter how egregious his actions were, and possibly still are.

I have said throughout this book that hurt people, hurt people. I have not one iota of doubt that you are grieving and in pain from your husband's choice to walk away from you and your marriage. You can list every fact, every complication, every consequence; and I would believe you.

On his end of the equation, he has his own list of justifications that he has used with his friends and others as to why he is without his wedding ring and living separate from his home. Wrong or right, valid or fabricated, truth or denial, understand that his mind only records what *he* wants to believe.

It doesn't matter.

Your husband may never offer you the validation of apology. He may instead continue to rattle off blame and his version of the story well into the future. Let God sort that out with him.

Within your own heart, you have the power to forgive, to flip the switch, and even to apologize for whatever it is he *feels* you have done.

Forgiveness, even one-sided, is an equalizer. It evens the score. It takes fault and blame, and neutralizes them so that the process of healing can begin. In the equation of right and wrong, when grace is added, the product is always peace.

Sometimes, this requires a whole lot more from one party, then the other. It will mean one of you needs to lead, extend, offer, accept, and forgive often way more than the other. However, if healing, if wellbeing, if reconciliation and peace is what you seek, then be *that* person.

It doesn't mean that all of a sudden, life is all moonbeams and cherries. It doesn't mean that everything goes back in place, and you kiss and make up. Although, if that is what happens, that is wonderful!

No matter what your relationship ultimately looks like, without forgiveness by at least one of you, it will never look different than it is now. You will always be chained and in bondage to the hurt that you already have. Time will not take it away. Only grace will.

Even in the worst of situations, suffering and consequences, God expects us to forgive. He *expects* us to. Sometimes, that means letting go just one finger at the time.

Our hearts, our spirits, our families, our provision, anything that has been damaged can be restored; but not until we release our burdens to Him. Not until we forgive.

Whether your husband ever apologizes to you is irrelevant. Whether or not he accepts *your* apology for your part of the transgression is not important. Certainly, we seek that validation, but we cannot depend on it.

We have to forgive him anyway.

The roots of bitterness can choke us off from life. They close us off from the harvest of blessings that come to us by the fruit of the Spirit. Joy, peace, and happiness are just a few.

Releasing your husband or anyone who has hurt you in the past or present, in love and forgiveness, opens us up to them again.

Even after all the hurt he caused. Even in the face of all the uncertainty tomorrow brings.

Grace is God's gift to us. It is ours to give *and* to receive. Grace is a spiritual ointment that helps us close the gaps of our wounds and begin the process of returning to normal again, even if normal looks different now.

Some people just don't forgive. They don't know how or choose not to. They use bitterness like a weapon, and it motivates them for all sorts of reasons. It becomes their idol. This, I assure you, will never lead to the endings they desire. Lives are ruined in a cyclone of trauma and drama to the point of utter destruction.

In our brokenness, we are fueled by misplaced desire to empty our verbal, emotional, and even legal guns out across the fence that divides us like the Hatfield's and McCoy's.

It's exhausting. It's depleting.

God asks us simply to get on our knees and let Him do the fighting for us.

Jesus was nailed to the cross to take away our sins. He endured it so that we could be free from the burden of darkness and a cursed life. When we refuse to forgive others, it is like taking God's sacrifice and giving it back to Him. We assume our own crucifixion. Inside, we bleed, gasp, and strangle the life within us. That's how destructive bitterness is.

God freely forgave us on the cross so that we could be made new. So that we could be made whole. It is the *only* love that comes with never having to say you're sorry. He gave it to us without our even asking Him.

I know that right now, you don't feel whole or new.

You feel as though you've been beaten up, forced into this situation against your will. Your belongings are being divided up; lots are being cast. What justice could come from such humiliation?

Jesus knows a thing or two about it. He knows your woe, and He is working to make it better.

> *Father, forgive them, for they do not know what they are doing. (Luke 23:34)*

You may never hear the words you want to hear from your husband. Forgive him anyway.

God is speaking directly to your heart. "I love you. I'm sorry. I'll take it from here." He means it, and that is His story of a love that never ends.

> *But the fruit of the Spirit is love, joy, peace, forbearance, kindness, goodness, faithfulness, gentleness and self-control. Against such things there is no law. (Gal. 5:22–23)*

11

The Cup

I DRINK TEA. LIVING IN the South, this usually means a tall glass of succulent sweetness poured over ice, and served with lemon and a straw. However, I am referring to the hot steaming kind, regular black pekoe in a tea bag, steeped for just the right number of seconds before it gets too dark. Add a teaspoon of sugar, stirred, not shaken. Clad in my bathrobe and slippers before everyone gets up, I'm a happy gal. Pretty predictable.

This is the time of day I love most. Sitting in the same spot on my couch, the Word opened on my lap, next to me are my agenda and my journal. I get to *think* in this space, unlike any other time in the day. Like my tea, I drink it deeply in. It's what keeps me sane, grounded, and prayerful.

I have this beautiful cup that I had bought maybe ten years ago from a Christian bookstore. I gave it to myself for Christmas. A simple white cup. In lovely, black calligraphy printed on the outside, it says, "Love ~ 1 Corinthians 13:8." On the inside brim where you can't avoid seeing it when taking a sip, it says, "Love Never Fails."

I love this cup. We go way back, me and it. Countless mornings, shuffling kids off to school, my husband off to work, myself juggling mascara and a load of dirty laundry thrown into the washer, and taking that last swig while filling up the dog's water bowl. Sometimes, this cup and I would sit at bedside, touching a warm, feverish forehead while a child slept, deciding if a visit to the doctor was warranted. Or sit cross-legged on the couch near my husband as we talked about some pressing need, problem or wish, or nothing at all.

Oh, the stories this cup could tell.

For the past year and a half, I noticed an empty pang inside of me, unaware of the reason I have chosen among other cups when standing at my counter first thing in the morning. After lunch too, when work keeps me chained at my desk and I need a quick seventh inning stretch and a shot of caffeine, it still sits banished to the back of the cabinet.

It finally dawned on me why I had adopted others that were fine in their own perfunctory way, though they offer nothing special, unlike my favorite cup.

It's a bit embarrassing to admit this. I had no intention of black-balling this mug. Even though the wear and tear of the years produced a tiny chip, just below the outer lip, it still works perfectly well. Wonderfully, in fact.

But I understand now what causes me to reach past it. It's not that I stopped drinking tea. It's not that I stopped reading the Word from which came the simple, amazing, and powerful quote. I thirst for it, eager to quench my spiritual pallet, just as my mouth absorbs that first, delicious sip of hot tea each morning.

It's the memory of who I was when I used it.

It's crazy how even the slightest reminder still can stick us like pins in a pin cushion. We avoid them, blindly deciding to not to go places like certain restaurants that we used to go to with him. We won't watch certain movies or listen to music by artists we used to like because hearing a particular song will cause us to unravel. Our minds so easily drift back to that once upon a time before our world got so harried and difficult.

Time now has a new distinction that it never had before. BHL and AHL—*Before He Left* and *After He Left*.

BHL represents the old you. BHL is still a bit painful to think about. BHL, I was a mom, a wife, the queen of my castle. I was happy, or so I thought. We had issues just like every family does, but we were whole and able to withstand it all. Love sustained us. It was real. It was unconditional, and the Scripture facing me each morning confirmed what I already knew.

AHL, I'm still figuring all this stuff out. I mean, what if all those years of believing the words I read on my favorite cup was really all a lie? *Love never fails.* Or does it?

People fail us. Our cars fail inspection. A kid comes home after studying all night for a test and worries if she will pass or fail. Our minds fail us sometimes, when we think wrong about someone or can't remember exactly what is in a recipe our grandmother used to make. We fail when we forget to mail out the water bill and it's already three days late. Gadgets that we buy don't always live up to the hype and fail.

Love gets damaged a bit, for sure. *We* get damaged a bit, and the lenses that we look at love through sometimes need to change. Our hearts expand or contract; they overflow or ache. But they keep right on beating from our first until our last breath.

Therefore, what would cause us to turn, to shy away even, from the simple reminders that love is a constant in our lives even when we might not be presently "in" it?

The answer, I believe, is in the Scripture itself. *Fail.*

We *believe* that love succeeds over all. It fixes all that is broken. It wards off evil and makes amends. It melts the hearts of the most uncaring people, causing perfect strangers to turn and help another without even a second thought. Even in the wild, animals show love and attachment.

It's the stuff of sappy movies where boy meets girl, falls for girl, loses girl, and then runs through a busy airport just in the nick of time to catch girl before she hands her ticket to the flight attendant and disappears forever.

Love is a many splendored thing. It binds us together. It makes life worth living.

Maybe *we* are just the exception. Maybe life doesn't get segmented into BHL and AHL for women who are more beautiful, more capable, more worthy than we are. Maybe our cups should just come with the added inscription on the other side: *"Love Never Fails . . . Unless your love isn't good enough to keep him."*

Even though this is *not* what my once favorite cup says, I can tell you, it didn't have to. I subconsciously said it to myself every time I used it, so I stopped. I just stopped.

There are a lot of reasons why we do this. Despite counselors, sermons, books, and Scripture, despite every person you know and love who assures you otherwise, there has to be someone to blame. Our minds want to understand the reason for our pain and disappointment. They search for meaning, for the origin, and conclude the only logical explanation. It must be *our* fault.

Somewhere along the line, *we* failed.

I have this knack for attracting thoughts that randomly come into my head. They are completely unrelated to anything I am going through in my life, or so I think. They are incongruent fragments that stick to my mind like Velcro until I peel them off and look at them. Sometimes, it's a song lyric, or the byline from an old commercial. Weird, odd things.

This happened to me a few months ago, right around the time I self-diagnosed my mug aversion. "Burn the ships!" Over and over, this came to me to the point of utter frustration. I couldn't understand it. I mean, I knew what it meant, and I had a pretty good understanding of what I was to take from it; but why would it not leave me? I pondered it for a few days and then Googled the origin of the phrase.

It seems that in 1519, Hernan Cortes arrived onto the shores of the New World with six hundred men. They disembarked, and immediately, Cortes ordered the ships to be burned. He heralded that they would either conquer the land before them or be killed. There was no turning back!

Cortes intended for his men to know that he was committed to achieving what they came to do. Destroying the ships assured that there would be no retreat. Fearful though they might have been, they were going forward by faith and a determined spirit toward their destiny.

A similar story is told about Elisha. When the cranky old prophet, Elijah, was told by God to find Elisha and anoint him, he set out to do so. Elisha was to succeed Elijah in serving God. As expected, younger Elisha was found plowing his field with twelve pairs of oxen. Elijah took off his cloak and threw it around him. The young prophet-in-training seemed to know what that meant. With barely a question, Elisha turned, slaughtered his yoke of oxen, and then burned his plowing equipment to cook the meat and distribute it to the people. With that, he then "set out to follow Elijah and become his attendant."

Failure was not an option. It makes you wonder, *How could they be so sure?*

When we said, "I do," didn't we also burn a ship or two? A plow, maybe? We gave up our last name and hitched our stars to the man we were yoked with. We had God's blessing and a vow to prove it. We had no intention of looking back but moved headlong into the future with a song in our heart and forever in our eyes. Love was the only option.

So why are we now shipwrecked on the Isle of Broken Dreams?

The truth is, we can't possibly know.

We can name things, point to things, work through things, but we still won't know until we arrive down the beach a ways, far enough to where God can reveal it all to us

"That is why I let you go through that. I know it didn't feel like it at the time, but I had a purpose for it, so you would be blessed, and everything would be made new. I needed you to trust me. See what I have done?"

More than ever, we must trust the plans He has for us.

After AHL, there will be a new season, and only God knows the acronym for it. One thing I do know is that it can and will be better than we can possibly imagine! There is grace there and the return of joy.

Love succeeds. Love flows. Love heals. Love hurts sometimes, but it doesn't fail.

Marriages do. Love doesn't.

Communication does. Expectations do. The road of righteousness has wrong turns that lead to sin. But all these things, when pursued in love, can be corrected and worked out so that we succeed in them.

Things fail. Technology, medicines, politics, making idols of money or pursuing dreams not rooted in well doing, all have failure within them.

We walk a fine line, a precipice. The line between good and evil, right and wrong. Love and hate.

The truth about the cup, my cup, is that it represents a time for me when life was simple. It's not that the cup failed me, but maybe I felt I had failed *it*. That somehow, I no longer felt that I was able to live the praise that the Scripture on it so boldly proclaimed. Maybe it was that I felt, in my circumstance, that although love didn't fail, it also hadn't exactly succeeded either.

AHL will do that to you.

The path we are on is laden with all kinds of land mines. One wrong step and we feel as though we may explode. We are taunted constantly to turn back, to not proceed in faith, to give in. We label ourselves, or allow others to, causing us to believe the untruths laid at our feet and in the deepest recesses of our minds.

Your love wasn't good enough to keep him.

Lies, lies and more lies.

We only fail, when we fail to love.

There was an old song from 1970 by Stephen Stills that was redone by a few different artists. It had the hook, "If you can't be with the one you love, love the one you're with." Maybe there is truth in this little ditty.

Love yourself, your friends, your family, your kids, your dog and cat, your neighbor, yes, even the crazy one. Love your coworkers and the lady at the fruit stand who reminds you of your great Aunt Edith. And if the one you love is not with you, it's not because you failed. It's not because love failed. It's because someone broke the terms that came with a covenant. That is something that comes with a hefty price.

It's a funny thing about that word, "unconditional." It's only good until it's not anymore. Until someone violates it. But God's love is. He has a covenant with us that cannot be broken.

The one who trusts in him will never be put to shame. (1 Pet. 1:6)

No matter what, God's love never fails us. Our love for others doesn't either. As long as it is rooted in Him, as long as it is held in the pure light of the promise that God is always working out what is best for those who love Him, we can love unconditionally. We can love even when the covenant that binds us to others has been shattered.

We can love someone from a distance and still hold them close in our hearts and prayers. We can still honor them, remembering the good parts, the cherished memories that don't fade with time. They played a part in the story of our lives, and we stand before God grateful for them. Loving doesn't have to mean you live with them. It doesn't mean that you still make them dinner and empty their pockets before throwing their dirty jeans in your washing machine.

We just don't know all of what our new season holds for us yet.

If we love and trust God's unconditional promises to us, His word, we can have the hope that's an anchor for our souls and that will not drift. It will not be returned void.

God burned the ships for us. There is no turning back. Where He is taking us is good land, filled with the promise that He will never leave us. There will be things in this new land that we must overcome. There will always be uncertainty, difficulty, perhaps a bit of grief that still touches us from time to time. But if we are armed with trumpets of faith and of righteousness, the walls that seem to hold us back and keep us hurting will come tumbling down.

God's scoped out this new land for us already.

We are already changed by what has happened to us. Even if tomorrow or next week, or next year, the miracle you are seeking and praying for comes, you will still be a different person than the one who existed before your husband left.

What we have endured is cloaked in hardship, but who we become, upon landing on this new shore, can inspire us to be the very best version of ourselves.

We will learn much here. We will conquer. We will forge ahead, not absent of fear, but driven ever greater by our faith in Who is leading us. No matter what, we are not the same people now, and that's okay.

We can come through these days in the desert in weeks or months, or forty years. The choice is ours. We can fail the test or succeed in the testimony at all that God has done within us and for us.

In a perfect world, we would not have been on the ship that delivered us to this new place. Everything would have remained the same, but that's not how life goes.

The seas get choppy. Dogs bite. Checks bounce. Husbands leave. We have to dig deep. We have to find the strength to no longer fear being reminded of who we used to be. We need to get out our favorite cup and drink from it with gusto.

Burn the ship. You are making great progress in this uncharted territory toward your destiny.

Love never fails. Never. No matter what.

> *Finally, all of you, live in harmony with one another; be sympathetic, love as brothers, be compassionate and humble. Do not repay evil for evil or insult with insult, but with blessing, because to this you were called. (1 Pet. 3:8–9)*

You are wondering, I know
If I can hear you when you pray
But I am with you
And sense, well beyond what your words ask of me,
All that you need
I feel your Faith
When it pulls me closer
Or when it wanes
And I am patient
I listen
As you seek out consolation from others
Some of these I have given to you
So that in their way
They will point you back to Me again
I notice
All the times your heart seems to break
Your tears flow
Or you hit the limit of what you believe
You can survive
And I understand
When you think that I have left you
All alone
What I can only tell you now
Is that this Season too shall pass
Lean on Me
I can hear you when you pray
And though you are wondering
What good can come of trials such as these?
Be comforted—
I know.

From the author's journal

12

The Shoe

M Y GRANDMOTHER TOLD A story of her older sisters when they were old enough to court gentlemen during the time of the Great Depression. They lived in a large family home with a wrap-around porch in a small Connecticut town. As resources were scarce, her sisters bartered, shared, and swapped their shoes among them so when male friends came calling on a summer Saturday night, the girls could tuck one worn, ugly shoe under their skirts and put one stylish, "good" shoe out in front. I am pretty certain that my grandmother's wonderful French-Canadian-New-England-American family did not come up with the phrase, "putting your best foot forward." It does, however, give quite a testimony to the ingenuity of young, eligible women wanting to make a good impression. It's a story I will never forget.

As I have shared, my grandmother was a huge influence in my life. She knew how to glean, seeing the best in people, life, and situations. She would save the most interesting remnants of things, spools of wire and twine, metal brackets, knobs and what-nots. When something needed fixing, she would pull out a box of these random items, many of them stored neatly in old glass jars. She knew *exactly* what to use and what would work when anything, from a rocking chair to a meat grinder, needed mending. She was the MacGyver of her time.

I'm sure that the Depression had its hand in teaching valuable lessons on making do with less as well as how to stretch a dollar. Frugality has its place when times are tough, but my grandmother and those great-aunts that I know of through stories shared and distant memory were very industrious and generous women. They sewed, crafting beautiful quilts from scrap pieces of fabric. They made delicious, big family meals, and everyone was welcome. They pulled together and did what they must in tending to their lives and families. Nothing was ever wasted.

This was a time when people knew where they came from and never forgot it. Their word was their bond, and gratitude for what they had came naturally. They were wealthy in that they had each other. My grandmother was the youngest of ten, and as each sibling moved from the courting stage to marriage, for the most part, that culture survived to the next generation.

Recalling this story of the shoes recently, I was thinking about how easily we discard things that are seemingly of no use anymore. What we throw out so casually, no doubt would have been of tremendous value during the days my grandmother was a young girl, but it goes much deeper than worn-out shoes and scraps of fabric.

We sometimes throw out people too. We discard them, finding them no longer of use to us. Like the picked-over bones from a chicken dinner, we find little left there worth keeping, so we don't. We've all done it on some level, and we have had it done to us, present circumstance included.

I don't know why it's hard to accept that God can use even the broken pieces, the remnants, of who we are, but He does. God does not see them as worthless. Rather, He already knows how He will use what remains as the building blocks to restore us to even greater than we can hope for. I can prove it.

We are valuable to God. He knows us. He has plans and a purpose for us. All we have to do is trust Him to lead us. Unfortunately, however, we are conditioned to believe the opposite.

In the aftermath, our energies are spent surviving. We spin our wheels, trying to gain traction, but we are adapting to so many different feelings and directions. It's difficult to know if we are making real progress. We want to prove that we still have value but not sure how. Despite our every effort to break free, to believe God, rejection still lingers.

For some reason, it's easier for us to believe the pronouncements, the labels, the "failure" of relationship; and we tend to bear more of the responsibility for our broken conditions.

God has a knack for taking those very same pieces and places within us and rework them, putting them in proper order, and then creating a new masterpiece. From leftover chicken can be made the most delicious chicken soup.

In order to put distance between the "broken" us and the whole person we yearn to become, we seek a platform to stand on so that we can look out over the expanse of what has happened and put context to it. We are growing a spine again, and though we are still vulnerable, we want to project to the world that we have landed on our feet and are ready to begin moving on.

In the same breath, we are compelled to put bubble wrap around what our marriage meant to us, as if putting it in storage. We hold on to the good and discount the bad. We want to isolate it and keep it from being altered in any way. In the face of so much hurt and division, we want it all to finally stop.

The warring, the blaming, the battling for who is right, we want to believe does not represent what we knew as our lives. All of that, we think, existed *outside* the entity that was our marriage. In hindsight, we want to know that our marriage itself was good, solid even. It's just the fighting/jealousy/drinking (whatever it was for you) that brought it down. Separating the marriage from the tarnished relationship somehow keeps it sacred and allows for it to remain valid.

Therefore, anything that came as a result of your union can also not be devalued.

For me, when my husband spoke negatively of our marriage, he was really slinging arrows at me; and I valiantly took them. Better me than the covenant. Better me than the love that produced our kids. Better me than destroying the memories of all that was good, of all that I know was real, of all that held my world for thirty years.

At this stage, I found myself holding on to remnants of a man who used to be all the things I loved most, forgetting to add the blemishes, inconsistencies, betrayal, and the times of downright egregious behavior. I so easily dismissed those things, that underneath it all, I forgot that there was hidden an ugly shoe or two.

I wanted to take the scraps of what was my married life and make a quilt that would keep me warm in lonely moments so that I could look and touch what was beautiful, the good times, and wrap them around me. I wanted to keep my memories of the man that I knew, lovely and pristine. Reasonable as it seemed, doing so put my husband on a pedestal that he honestly no longer deserved. More than this, it kept me from healing.

This may sound conflicting. I have spent most of this book sharing about how we are to love each other, forgive, and remain open to God's will for us. We are to free ourselves from the traps that snare us in bitterness and resentment. And this is all true.

What I have come to understand is that, like finding our way out of a maze, there are plenty of wrong turns and bumping into walls. We look for an opening and want to believe it's a straight shot. It's not. Taking shortcuts means that we sometimes fail to notice at all the clues, and this only prolongs our exit out of pain and into true healing.

Another way of explaining this, for me, is that I was so used to compensating, to taking the burden and the blame, and carrying it solely on my shoulders that I was continuing to do so even after my husband left. It was as though I *had* to. This one-sided view didn't allow the perspective I needed to understand it all.

I think as women, we carry more of the burden than what rightfully belongs to us. We must learn to give it to God instead.

Does God want us to forgive and forget? Absolutely. But I have learned that forgiveness is also a *process* that we must walk through before we can fully forget.

God loves us unconditionally, warts and all. When we come to Him with our troubles, He doesn't wave a magic wand and expect all that we have done is to be washed away right along with our sins. He expects us to use what we've been through so that we can help others. He gives us grace, so that can turn around and offer the same.

> *The Father of compassion and the God of all comfort, who comforts us in all our troubles, so that we can comfort those in any trouble with the comfort we ourselves have received from God. (2 Cor. 1:4–5)*

Healing comes from wading through the good parts *and* the bad. It's holding up all the parts to the light and not glossing over them, not making excuses for them, but accepting them.

This takes time.

It's the same process when we take accountability for ourselves and our mistakes against others. It's what we must also do when others have made mistakes and hurt us.

Choosing to forgive can come in a heartbeat. But sometimes, it takes a little work to push the remnants from our hearts, emotions, and spirits.

It's not our job to determine if ultimately those that hurt us will take responsibility and repent for their wrongdoing. It is only our job to contend, to process, to carry on with all that affects us, our lives and our healing, so that we are not outside the will of God.

It's not a determination to love or not love, to forgive or not forgive. It's more a matter of giving yourself the space to realize that there were areas of conflict that grew and festered, and weren't always pretty. It's examining all of it, putting perspective around it, and then tucking it away, no longer to have power over us.

It's allowing you to put both shoes out there at the same time and be okay with the ugly and the good.

When we elevate our husband, as we tend to do when we miss someone, and think only of how wonderful he was and not reconcile the difficulties that he also may have brought to the relationship, in a sense, we make an idol of him. In doing so, we are not looking at the true picture of the man. Every man and woman comes with a set of faults and hypocrisies, and only God can help us with these.

We are all a work in progress. We do not cheapen or discount the sanctity of our marriage just because we admit the frailties and weaknesses within it. Doing so gives us clarity. Doing so makes us no longer the victim of abandonment, but the recipient of the blessings that will come as a result of what has happened. Doing so opens us up, preparing us for what comes next. Doing so takes the burden of blame and makes it an equation where solving for "x" makes all things equal.

The truth is that what happened changes us. All of us. We are transformed by enduring hardship, and I believe that, as a result, we become a better version of who we were. Even that which we consider the once "happy" version of ourselves. Having faith, and trusting God to be God, brings us to the understanding that there is still better for us to come. We *will* be happy again.

We did not elect to go through this, but the process has a purpose. If we do not grow weary, if we do not resist in letting God take us through it His way, that purpose will be revealed. Once we have traveled down the road a bit further, we will be able to look back and connect the dots. We will be able to see how He is setting us up to restore us.

You might not have been able to see what was coming with your husband, but God did. Though He didn't make it happen, he already has it handled. He is in this with you. Though you can't yet see it or imagine it, He is working it all out for you.

Like dross from silver, enduring the fire purifies us. The composition of who we are is being made into a stronger, deeply compassionate woman.

When we go without love, relationship, or connection, when we are tossed about in a life storm, we gain an appreciation for what is missing. We come out of it placing a greater value on people especially those that *do* love us. We gain even greater empathy and gratitude for what we have and what He is bringing us to.

When Ruth was encouraged by her mother-in-law, Naomi, to go back to her family rather than follow her to Bethlehem, she said no. Ruth and her sister-in-law, Orpah, were widowed by Naomi's sons, and Naomi herself was also a widow. Orpah took Naomi's advice and left to return to her family of origin in Moab.

However, Ruth would not leave. "Where you go, I will go and where you stay, I will stay. Your people will be my people and your God my God." She was steadfast, determined to do what was right in honoring her husband's mother and not breaking the covenant of that bond.

Naomi lamented at her misfortune and the condition in which she was returning to her homeland. "I went away full, but the Lord has brought me back empty."

I bet you can relate.

Ruth was Naomi's remnant. As they returned to Bethlehem, people took notice. And so did a man named Boaz.

Needing food, Ruth went into his field, asking to go behind the harvesters and gather little bits of whatever was left, spilled, or unpicked from their work. Boaz was a relative of Naomi's husband, Elimelech. In those days, respect and honor was given to the dead to the degree that the family had an obligation to consider redeeming Elimelech's good name and lineage by marrying into it. Boaz, it so happens, was Elimelech's kinsman redeemer.

Ruth's work paid off. She gathered enough barley to sustain her and Naomi. Because Boaz took kindly to her, remarking at her unselfish devotion to her mother-in-law, he shared with her an even greater portion. Ruth was putting her best foot forward, and Boaz was impressed.

Here she was, a widow, away from the land of her birth, but bound by love to a woman who felt empty at her losses; but Ruth remained. In the end, when Boaz realized her pure spirit and devotion, he married her.

Ruth could have cast aside the old woman, but she didn't. When she married Boaz, Naomi was also blessed to be enveloped once again into a thriving family. Ruth would have children, and from that lineage would come David. Many generations later, Joseph, a carpenter, would choose to not cast aside a teenaged girl to whom he was engaged and was said to be carrying a child that was not his, but God's.

Jesus was the remnant, born in a manger. He would grow to one day glean men, those looked over and thought of little value. He brought light, love, healing, and forgiveness to a fallen world. He brought redemption. He brought eternal life.

All of that could have been changed had one broken woman not gone to glean in a barley field. Because she endured, Ruth was transformed, and so aren't we all.

The world, as we know, is good at celebrating "victories." Football stadiums rock with enthusiasm when the home team wins. Bars fill up and raise glasses to all sorts of trivial milestones, only to have an excuse to party and carry on. Sin is exalted. Covenants are mocked as being unreasonable and controlling and are burned at the altar of being "free" and having "fun."

The serpent slithers to and fro, content in knowing that the deception is racking up victims for his side. The world says, "Good for me!"

Here we are, like Ruth, gleaning in the field of what is left behind, scratching the earth for what remains of us, our families, and completely uncertain of our futures. And God says, "Good for you."

Our endurance in these times is producing something in us and through us that will be rewarded a hundredfold.

One day, the Lord commanded Elijah to go to the town of Zarephath. He told the prophet that he would meet a widow there.

Destitute and hungry due to the famine, the woman was found just as the Lord said, and Elijah came to her as she was gathering kindling for a fire. He asked the woman for water and a piece of bread.

The woman replied, "As surely as the Lord lives, I don't have any bread—only a handful of flour in a jar and a little oil in a jug. I am gathering a few sticks to make a meal for myself and my son, that we may eat it—and die."

Elijah said to her, "Don't be afraid. Go home and do as you have said. But first make a small cake of bread for me, and then make something for yourself and your son." He wanted her to use her remnants. "For this is what the Lord, the God of Israel, says. 'The jar of flour will not be used up and the jug of oil will not run dry until the day the Lord gives rain on the land.'"

In obedience, the woman did what he said. The flour was not used up and the oil did not run dry. There was food every day for Elijah, the woman, and her family. What a way to test the broken pieces of a woman's faith.

It's easy, from this place, to look about the landscape in the aftermath of your storm and feel helpless. We tend to think that those who cast aside others, going headlong with gusto while thinking only of themselves, have it all. But life doesn't always work out like that.

Sin is seductive. Satan is the master manipulator, a director in a play that has unexpected plot twists, and a surprise ending that no one will like.

There are days we feel like we are gleaning and finding nothing. We need to glean anyway.

There are days when all we can find are two worn shoes to wear, and nothing that will impress a suitor of any kind. Wear them anyway. You never know who is watching you.

Much can be redeemed from what remains.

God gave favor to Ruth and to the old woman with the oil and flour. My grandmother's sisters married and thrived. Countless things were fixed and mended from odds and ends stored in a little box next to my grandmother's washing machine.

You and I have our own redemption stories too. God has us and will reward us in our enduring, transforming us, changing and mending us in all the right places. There is an ending to our stories that God has already written for us. The remnants of what is left are the seedlings for what is to come.

Perhaps, if it is His will, redemption can come in the return of a repentant, prodigal husband. If not, your Boaz is out there right now, asking God for a woman who will honor Him above all and who knows the value of a covenant. It's only a matter of time before your paths cross. Just keep putting one foot in front of the other and making it through each day in faith.

Sometimes, we are the blind leading the blind, but keep walking just the same. Start by putting your best foot forward.

Be grateful for the remnants. They are the very best part of what seems broken. You are a masterpiece.

Just watch what God does. He has a plan, and it will blow your socks off.

> But they who wait on the Lord shall renew their strength.
> They shall mount up with wings like eagles;
> they shall run and not be weary;
> they shall walk and not faint. (Isa. 40:31)

> The stone that the builders rejected has become the cornerstone. (Ps. 118:22)

13

Spurs

WHEN I WAS TEN, I fell off a horse and broke my arm. I couldn't tell you the name of my friend with whom I sat shotgun as she cantered the brown-and-white mare around the corral near where I lived in Chatsworth, California. All I can tell you is that when it happened, I knew it. I remember holding my right hand close against my abdomen as I climbed up two hilly embankments that were the shortcut back to my street. My mom wasn't home and, after sobbing for a bit, I fell asleep on the couch waiting for her. I was afraid to tell her what had happened. I didn't want to add more to her burdens, another bill, another reason to worry.

When she came in and found me, she wasn't mad at me like I thought she might be. She scooped me up and took me to the emergency room, and several hours later, I returned with a long plaster cast, bent ninety degrees at my elbow. The good news is that I had something for show and tell the next morning.

The thing about falling off a horse is that you need to get right back on it. You can't let a fall stop you. You've got to keep riding. Otherwise, fear takes over; and before you know it, you're too afraid to give it another try.

In my case, my friend and I weren't particularly close. It's possible that after breaking my arm, her folks were afraid that my mom would say it was their fault. All I know is that we never spent time together again. Another ride was not in the cards.

That was the year my brother went missing, my grandfather died, and my mom remarried a man, more out of necessity than love, that no one was fond of. Still, I managed to make it out of Mrs. Graves's fourth grade class relatively unscathed.

Up until now, we've covered some pretty big topics: loving people who've hurt us, forgiving when we can't forget, learning to put that one foot in front of the other. These are hard things to do when you feel not only like you've fallen off a horse, but kicked by one too.

I believe that our hearts, when healed enough, know instinctively how to love again. I believe the same about forgiveness. Time has a way of showing us that things work out the way they are supposed to. We somehow learn to accept what we cannot change.

Perspective gives us the blessing of seeing things that we once found too difficult to acknowledge. Either in our own persona or our husband's, we are circumspect of the conditions of our lives leading up to the breaking apart. These revelations are neither pleasant nor endearing, but they are profoundly important. They are guideposts for our healing. They help us to move on.

We all yearn to be loved again, and we become open to the possibility that it might well not be our husbands who are trusted with the role in doing so.

When the proprieties that come with officially ending a marriage occur, when sufficient time has passed, and you are sensing your readiness, the prospect of seeking a new relationship will propel you forward. (This does not exclude a "new" relationship with your husband if after healing and proper counseling/intervention this restoration is made possible.)

But questions remain. How do we know when it's safe to trust again? How do we get back on that horse?

Trust is the first thing to break and the last thing to heal.

The truth is that there are no guarantees in life. There is always risk. People we love the most will let us down. Our husbands, our parents, our friends, even our children from time to time. It's true of us as well. It's just how it works. We all make mistakes and fall from grace in little and big ways. Getting back up, dusting ourselves off, making amends, and forgiving where necessary put us back in the saddle.

When we think of those we trust, who have the integrity of their word and our best interest in mind, we feel safe just visualizing them. Our spirits hold them close to us with love, honor, respect, and gratitude without their even needing to speak. When we love and trust someone, there is unconditionality. When the chips are down, we believe without question that they will be there for us.

If over time, however, that trust is marginalized, bartered, negotiated to justify other interests, constantly drawing into question if that person is sincere, then the cracks in the foundation of that relationship are exposed.

Trust is comprised of other words that are its fruit; honesty, faithfulness, temperament, and commitment are just a few. It is this fruit by which we deem others as *trustworthy*. If the fruit of trust is damaged, then the whole foundation is compromised and corrupted. Every aspect of trust comes into question.

If, for example, someone we love is found to be unfaithful or dishonest, the trust that we have for them in all other aspects of relationship is fractured and diminished.

We can trust someone—a doctor, a colleague, a neighbor—and not be in a love relationship with them. We can also love someone and *not* trust them. True, intimate relationships, such as husband and wife, cannot survive without both trust *and* love.

Because we are not infallible, we will make mistakes. Trust can take a hit now and then; but it can be mended with grace, repentance, and rekindling over the rough patch. We do this often throughout our lives.

However, there comes a point when trust is so damaged, when repentance is mocked, when the integrity that once held the framework of relationship intact becomes undone. We are left then with only the *memory* of who he was, not the person himself. Even if he is still in some semblance of relationship, perhaps even living with you, who you *believed* him to be is very different from who he has become in your eyes.

When the fruits of trust no longer exist, the relationship is changed to the degree that it only occupies space. There is nothing to nurture it, nothing to breathe life back into it.

Only God can create within someone a new heart and a new spirit. From these, the fruit of trust will be reborn. Resuscitation of relationship is only truly possible when the bonds of trust are mended.

As women, we can give all the grace in the world. We can accept the promises of one who swears to make things right. We all yearn for reconciliation if at all possible. But God must be in it for it to work.

If your husband were to come home now and with tears in his eyes tell you how sorry he is for what he's done, that would no doubt move you. But without trust, you are only rewinding a movie you have already seen.

If God is orchestrating the comeback, you will see the fruits returning. You will *know* that it is real. The evidence will speak for itself.

Actions speak louder than words.

The season we are emerging from has left us hollow. Like the scarecrow in the *Wizard of Oz*, after the flying monkeys got ahold of him, his stuffing strewn everywhere, we must gather ourselves. "They tore my legs off and threw them over there! Then they tore my chest out and they threw it over there!"

Stuffing ourselves back together isn't easy, but we are managing. We are learning that we already have within us the brains, the heart, and the courage that we need. It's just learning to exercise them altogether to coordinate and sync up our lives again. That takes time.

We don't want to fall. The last thing we need right now is another broken arm.

Learning to trust again requires us putting one foot back in the stirrup, and leaping up and over in faith. It's sitting up there on the horse a while, getting your bearings and surveying what's around you.

When you're ready, when time and providence have done their jobs, you will give a little "giddy up" and start out at a nice, easy pace. Not a gallop, not even a trot. Just a slow and steady walk around the ranch to see how things look out there.

I hear that there are still some cowboys with white hats, and God has been working on them, just like He is working on you and me. The getting back on the horse is easy if we trust that He holds the reigns.

I know how hard it is when we still have unresolved feelings, when we still have love for our husbands, to go forward. We would rather stay in the corral, fearful of setting out again, afraid to risk exposing our vulnerability. Dysfunction, blame, breakdown, and whatever else our marriages became even seem preferable to venturing off to territories unknown.

We are conditioned to believe that the devil we know is better than the devil we don't know, but this kind of thinking keeps us stuck. It keeps us looking back, thinking that there must be some mistake that we can fix.

Samuel had a similar problem. He was the one who anointed Saul as Israel's first king. They went through a lot together, Saul and Samuel. They shared a covenant, a bond. God would use Saul for His purpose, and Samuel would help Saul to keep him in His will. It seemed like a pretty good arrangement. All Saul had to do was stay obedient to the Lord, and all would be well in the kingdom.

Then came this little episode with the Amalekites. Samuel told Saul *exactly* what the Lord said what was to happen and how Saul needed to handle it. He told him to go fight the Amalekites and then destroy all that belonged to them, sparing nothing, down to the sheep, camels, and donkeys.

As often happens in the face of difficulty, we start to second-guess God. We wonder if we can find gray areas, maybe to purposefully misinterpret. *Surely, God didn't mean everything! Couldn't we bend the rules just a bit? Maybe save a few lambs, a fatted calf or two?* Saul and his men had done *most* of what God had asked. What harm would a little disobedience do?

The Lord came to Samuel, grieved at what had happened because Saul "has turned away from me and has not carried out my instructions." Samuel also was troubled and "cried out to the Lord all that night."

Oh, the cost of sin. It always ruins a good thing. It causes a ripple—a mere pebble dropped in the middle of still water meant to be undetected. Soon, a wave can be seen from the shore.

Consequences always come.

Samuel went to visit Saul. "What is this bleating of sheep in my ears?"

Saul was ready with his justifications. He explained how he had done what the Lord asked of him. He and his men took only the good plunder—the best of the animals—"but totally destroyed the rest."

However, the damage was done. Samuel told Saul what God would do. He would no longer be king.

Samuel mourned Saul. He loved him; they had history. But Saul could no longer be trusted.

You can feel his disappointment, can't you? You can feel how Saul let Samuel down. It was only a little thing, a few sheep, but he broke the covenant. He blew it.

Being in the time before Jesus would come and reconcile the hearts of men, there was only one consequence. God removed the favor He had placed on Saul's life. He turned His back on him. This must have devastated Samuel.

God said to him, "How long will you mourn for Saul, since I have rejected him as king over Israel? Fill your horn with oil and be on your way; I am sending you to Jesse of Bethlehem. I have chosen one of his sons to be king." He wanted Samuel to get back on the horse.

I don't know about you, but I have great empathy for Samuel. He barely had time to pick up his chin and then go start all over again with someone new. He had to find someone to take the place of the one he loved. He had to forge a new covenant, and his heart was barely healed.

I've heard of people in similar situations. I bet you have too.

It's hard to trust again when our hearts have been broken, when we've been betrayed. It's hard to come out of our cave to endure the light of day and carry on as if everything is fine. Can we trust another ever again?

It's hard to believe that someone else won't also blur the lines of right and wrong, getting away with just a little tiny lie, a little pinch of sin, or find the celebration of the plunder more fun than hanging out with you.

It's hard too trusting that God knows what's ahead for us. But He does.

I cannot tell you how many times I ask this question of myself, particularly when I am having a difficult moment. Like when I look around at social occasions or I notice all the couples in the movie theater on a Saturday night, and I am by myself. I ask it when it feels like my Boaz got my address mixed up with someone else's and has no GPS to find me.

Do I trust God? *Yes, Lord, I trust you.*

Saul told Samuel when offering his excuse, "I was afraid of the people, and so I gave in to them." Saul chose the world's ways over God's.

True repentance—turning away from sin, turning away from caring what the world says, and doing only what God would have us do—is the key. God can heal us, make us whole, reconcile our differences, reunite us for His glory. Love can endure the breach of covenant if God is in the mending of it. God loves these endings, and so do we.

But the character of a man, *without* repentance, causes his word and integrity to become void. How can such a man be trusted again? I ask you to think about this, as I have had to countless times.

Even though Samuel's heart still longed for the man he knew best, who was more trustworthy? Saul or the man that Samuel would anoint next? After going to meet Jesse, he looked over all his sons; and not satisfied, he asked if there were any others. *Yes, there is still the youngest.*

Jesse didn't think that Samuel would like him. He smelled kind of bad, being out with the sheep, and he had a ruddy complexion. Certainly, the other brothers, especially the tall, dark, and handsome Eliab, would have more to offer than little ol' David.

Do I trust God? Samuel must have asked. *Yes, Lord, I trust you.*

When David entered the home, God told him what to do. "Rise and anoint him. He is the one."

Not only would David become the greatest of kings, but he did so because he had a heart for God. He would put Him first in all things. Though he was not perfect, his repentance was true, and so was his faithfulness. He bore good fruit.

I wish there was a test that we could do to check when our hearts are ready to trust again. Whether it is our husbands who come back, saying all that one would need to say, or just the guy with the nice smile who asked you to coffee.

But there is not. There is only faith.

There is only our believing that God's hand is on us. There is only the knowing that He wants us to be loved, honored, and protected.

Will we hear a voice like Samuel? "*Rise—he is the one.*" Will we know if he has a heart for God? If God is in it, we will know.

He gives us intuition. He gives us grace. He will give us confirmation when it is right. It will be well with our soul.

Before you get back on the horse, back in relationship, don't be afraid to look him in the eyes and tell him, "You know, I got hurt once on a horse like you. I want to trust that you won't take off running. I want to know that you will take care so that I do not fall."

If his heart is for the Lord, he will do just that.

From the beginning of time, people who should have been trusted with the hearts and interests of others, fell. But God always has a way of turning things for our good.

Joseph's brothers threw him into a pit, and Joseph rose to save all of Egypt from the famine. Queen Vashti refused King Xerxes's request to join him at the banquet, so Esther was made queen, and she would save the Jews from Haman's plot to destroy them. And Jesus, betrayed by Judas, would die on the cross, rise again in three days, and bring us salvation and eternal life.

It's true; we do not know the terrain ahead. Trust that God knows the way. Trust that you are being restored in all the right ways with nothing broken, nothing missing.

Trust that the plans He has for you are to provide for you, prosper you, and restore you. He wants to lead you to true healing, love, and the return of joy to your life.

To finish off the story of my fourth-grade year, I offer you this footnote. About a week or two after getting my cast off my arm, my appendix ruptured while at the home of another friend whose house I was at with some other girls for a sleepover. The house, it so happens, was the ranch formally owned by Roy Rogers and Dale Evans. Though they were a little before my time, I knew that they were a pretty big deal. They were America's original God-loving cowboy couple. There was a game room with a pool table, and on the floor were the initials RR and DE. I remember this because I was up most of the night, pacing around that room, waiting for first light.

I was down for several weeks after emergency surgery. I finished out the school year and went along as usual to spend the summer with my grandparents. I was thin; the wear and tear of all I had been through that season was evident. With love, rest, and some fresh air, I was restored in all the right ways.

It will happen for you too. Fill your horn with oil and be on your way. Get back on that horse and ride, girl.

Happy trails.

14

Jericho

THERE IS A PLACE between vindication and victory that I am standing in right now. Certainly not all things are perfect, but God is providing for me. Miraculously. Amazingly. I am seeing that what lies before me is just as wonderful as what was behind, and maybe even better.

The length of time that it has taken you to read these pages, I would guess is not as long as it has taken me to write them. In saying that, you might still be deep in the valley from which I am finally emerging. If so, I pray you will be coming out soon as well.

Like Caleb, sent by Moses, along with his fellow scouts to explore the Promised Land, let me guide you a bit.

I know that the Desert of Despair has been a difficult place. But where we are heading is a good land; a land of peace, of prosperity of spirit, of healing. It's the place that God has promised all of us who love Him and seek His ways.

There will be many who will want to tell you differently. They will warn you about what's ahead, about others who will want to do you harm. They may even caution you not to get your hopes up, to be practical, and to be on the lookout for the "players" out there who want only one thing; and you best not think they won't try to get it. You are, after all, single again. Better be prepared! Your best days, they might suggest, are in the past. They will spread a bad report.

In the battle of your own mind, all the words, all the blame, and all the misdeeds will follow you. You will see lack, your rusty social skills, and worry how you will go out and create a new life. It will seem even reasonable to believe the musings of those who want to discourage your progress.

Before us, there might be Canaan, but there are things that we have to get through before we can claim the land as ours.

The problem with those who explored the land, all except Caleb and Joshua, was that they focused on the obstacles, not the promise. They saw the giants among the people there, but they never stopped to consider how big their God was. As if God would not equip them to handle whatever came their way.

When they returned from their expedition, the men went around the camp, doing all they could to squash any thoughts of going to the Promised Land. At one point, they even advocated stoning Caleb and Joshua to death, afraid that they would cause an uprising. They thought it best to stay put and not venture out. They wanted to play it safe.

"The land that we explored devours those living in it."

Caleb and Joshua saw beyond the dangers. They believed God would not send them into a land that He had not already prepared them for.

My favorite book as a young child was *The Little Engine That Could* by Watty Piper. Using visualization, the little blue steam engine, overcame incredible odds. She chose not to compare her diminutive size to those hefty engines around her. Instead, she focused on her heart and her spirit.

"I think I can, I think I can, I think I can, I think I can." Up the mountain she climbed, all the way to the top.

The image of this book has stayed with me all my life. I can't tell you how many times, in the face of great difficulty, I needed to summon whatever core strength I had. I heard the words of this prose repeated endlessly, but they came to me more like the words of a prayer.

"I know I can. I know I can. I know I can do all things through Christ who strengthens me." And many, many times, I did. I overcame and made it. I climbed that proverbial mountain to the top.

I wish that I could write something here that would cause you the same simple motivation to see, not the giants that you are facing in this new Land of Oneness, but yourself as an overcomer. We all have a little engine inside of us. It's sometimes just a matter of learning how to stoke the fire within and build up the steam to pull ahead. It's a matter of belief, not just that *you* can, but that He will give you the strength to do so.

I've read a lot in this season that we are surviving together. Inspiration comes in all kinds of images and statements of faith. I love to see snippets and reminders of what God has placed within each of us—a tremendous capacity to do well beyond what we think we are capable. We are so much more than the labels we have inherited or accepted. Our endurance, our stamina, though sometimes in need of replenishment, always astonishes me.

What we have already pushed ourselves through has taken a toll, but do you know what? Here we are, ready to see what else God has in store. All we need to do is cross over. The naysayers can stay where they are.

I know that you probably don't feel victorious. There are a lot of issues yet to settle. There are boxes to pack or unpack—emotionally, fiscally, physically. In many ways, you are already in a new land. Your domain has been changed. Your domicile looks nothing like the way it started out.

But you're still standing.

I will admit to you that there are moments that still catch me. I will wake up in the middle of the night or attend a function with one of my kids, and I am brought to a surreal anomaly of my womanhood. I *was* one-half of two. Now, I am one whole of one. I am just me.

There are still questions left unanswered. There are still fragments of emotion that trip me up. But I want to be Caleb, not all the others who tell me the reasons why I can't go forth and claim my future and all that God has for me.

Caleb must have heard the story of the little engine too. He tried to encourage the people by what he saw. "We should go up and take possession of the land, for we can certainly do it."

The Israelites grumbled, unwilling to move beyond the place that they were in. Fear gripped them and held them bound. Caleb and Joshua tried to convince them that the land was exceedingly good and to have faith in God who promised it.

They refused to believe. Their lack of faith cost them ever seeing what God so desperately wanted to give them. They would never set foot in the land of good fruit, of milk and honey. Instead, they would wither on their own vine of bitterness. They would remain in the desert for the rest of their days.

I can't think of a sadder ending for all those who *wanted* to believe but were silenced by the crowd to not do so. They got overruled, made to feel foolish that they could have the good that God had promised them. Their voices were drowned out by others that said they could not surmount the obstacles ahead. The desert was their lot, and they just would have to deal with that.

I bet there were women who would go out secretly, holding their baskets and jars, overlooking the land of Judah from the Valley of Jericho to the City of Palms. I wonder how many of them said, "If it were up to me, I would go there. I would find a way. I would claim the land."

I know I would have been one of them.

The hardest part of crossing the Jordan, that strip of ourselves that still lingers from the shore of What Was to the other side of What Will Be, is fear.

What if everything we were told was "wrong" about us is true? What will we lose if we completely let go? Who will follow us into our new season? What if we want to come back?

When we started out on this journey, we were still living in the land of Pharaoh. Yes, we had our daily provision, but we were subjects of a man who didn't appreciate the value of who we were. We gave it all we had. We worked hard. We were loyal, eager to please, and our hearts were for doing what was right. We honored the man and the covenant that held us.

But God knew that a change was coming.

It might not have been the ten plagues that came, but there were breaches, warnings of one sort or another. We could excuse some, others not so much. All the while our station in life was attached to someone who, whatever his reasoning, would leave us.

His exodus was in the making, and we just didn't see it coming.

God gave us what we would need. Manna, quail, water that would flow from a rock. All came to us disguised as other things: Friends who encouraged. Doors that opened before us. Sustenance and provision that miraculously showed up to keep us going. He covered us with a cloud of His presence, if only to remind us that He too was on this journey.

He has never ever left us.

It wasn't easy for the Israelites to leave Egypt. That was the only life they knew. Change is never comfortable. But there was this guy named Moses, staff in hand, taking them away with the vague understanding that God would deliver them somewhere new.

Their grumbling caused the trip to go on much longer than necessary. God was not just trying to get the Israelites out of Egypt, but He was trying to get *Egypt* out of the Israelites.

They did not cooperate. They kept looking back. They doubted. They took the blessings that He had provided along the way for granted. They stopped believing better would come.

For too long, this describes me as well. How about you?

All God wanted was for them to activate their faith. He wanted to hear, "I think He can. I know He will."

We can't know all that our new season, our new land, holds for us. All we know is that to grumble about it will ruin it for us. We must instead look for what is coming with expectation that it is good.

Finally, after forty years of what it was said should only have taken eleven days, Joshua would gather up the remnants of his people and lead them across the Jordan. He would take them to the land long promised to them.

The Lord told Joshua, "Today I will begin to exalt you in the eyes of Israel, so that they may know that I am with you."

I love that God said, "*begin* to exalt you." To me, that meant that His favor was not an event, but a commitment that He would not leave him in all that was to come. God was with him because of Joshua's faith and obedience.

When Joshua set foot in the Jordan, its waters flowing downstream were held back so that the Israelites could safely cross. God was making a way were there was no way.

In the middle of it, Joshua would command the twelve men he had appointed. "Each of you is to take up a stone on his shoulder, according to the number of tribes of the Israelites, to serve as a sign among you. In the future, when your children ask you, 'What do these stones mean?' tell them that the flow of the Jordan was cut off before the ark of the covenant of the Lord. When it crossed the Jordan, the waters of the Jordan were cut off. These stones are to be a memorial to the people of Israel forever."

We have stones too that we carry. Memories, experiences, blessings that we are reluctant to leave behind. As women, we think that our moving into our new seasons means that we are supposed to forget what was our past. We can't. God doesn't expect that of us. These things are the monuments of our lives—the parts of our story, our loves, our losses. They can never be forgotten. They have shaped us.

We don't one day just decide to turn our back on our former lives. We can't move to our next season without considering how we got there. We honor all that preceded, and what it all meant to us. Even the difficult parts. That's just the way it works.

There is a difference between looking back, longing for what was, and looking forward while perhaps still grieving the parts of us that hurt. It's a process, not a permanent condition. We are made up of all of our experiences. The good, the bad, and the ugly. They come with us wherever we go. Just like the cars of a train, they follow us. Just like the little engine that could.

Faith is believing in our hearts what we are praying for, but it is also walking it out. It is actively proclaiming what we believe God has for us.

After they crossed the Jordan, when they got to Jericho, the Lord told Joshua how to march around the walls of the city. For seven days, that's what they did. They stopped grumbling. They were obedient. At the ready, when Joshua gave the signal by way of a trumpet blast, all the men knew to give a mighty shout!

When the moment came, the sound of their voices filled the air and the walls of Jericho came tumbling down. The Israelites had announced their triumph! They witnessed their victory as the walls, the barriers to the city, let loose before them.

I bet they were astonished. I bet they jumped up and down, high-fiving one another.

They made it! They entered their new land. They defeated not just the enemy, but also their own fears.

What will you do when you arrive in your new season? When you feel you no longer have to prove who is right, who is wrong? When you know, soundly, that God has removed you from a place where you were not fully loved, acknowledged, or appreciated?

It's hard to imagine what the Promised Land looks like, but I'm starting to get glimpses. I can sense a place where, thinking about what is behind me, no longer aches, no longer causes me to cower in broken unbelief. I am free to believe what I want about myself, about others, and about my God. He is bigger than any giant I have ever had to deal with.

God knew what my former season was like, long before I did. He saw what I could not see. Though I would have been content to carry on in it, the Ruler of my life thought differently. He knew that leaving Egypt would not be easy, but He knew that it would be worth it. And that is enough.

Let those who grumble stay on the far side of the Jordan where nothing ventured means nothing gained.

My toes are in the water, and I am crossing over. Who is coming with me?

You are a brave, mighty little engine. With God, all things are possible. Focus on the cadence of your healing heart, and step on in.

"I think I can, I think I can, I think I can."

I *know* you can.

15

My Heart Still Sings

THERE IS AN OLD Barry Manilow song, "I Can't Smile Without You," that I remember from when my husband and I first started our relationship. It had been out for several years before we knew each other, but I recall vividly hearing it, along with a few other songs he recorded, and thinking, "Yeah, that's the way I feel. I can't imagine my life without you."

When we met, I was living in Orange County, California, and he was living near Boston, where he had grown up. In the days before you could go on YouTube and forward songs by text to each other, my husband had rigged up something on his landline telephone so that he could play music for me that went along with our budding romance. "Time in New England" was another favorite.

It's funny, when I hear these songs now randomly, in a doctor's office or restaurant, how differently they affect me. What was once so endearing, so special, now only underscores the opposite meaning. The words are still the same, but the interpretation is 180 degrees the other extreme.

You know I can't smile without you
I can't smile without you
I can't laugh, and I can't sing
I'm finding it hard to do anything.

The song that had reflected the yearning of a heart newly in love, now is the sentiment of a chapter that is closing with a very different ending indeed. Yet the words still fit somehow.

Music is amazing in how it transports us back in time. We can remember so vividly, in such detail, things that we might otherwise not think about. A song can transport us instantly to a land far, far away.

Writing this book, sharing my story with you, was a little bit like this. The words are what they are, but they will mean something very different depending on where you are sitting on the spectrum of this journey.

For me, they allowed me to reach back and tie up some loose ends. I can understand better where wounds were caused and better sense the healing that never commenced. So much gets buried, swept under the rug, and is never dealt with. We think, as though children, that out of sight is out of mind. But that is never, ever the case.

Wounds that are not healed, fester. They get infected and can come back to harm us even decades—even lifetimes—after they occurred.

When the world's solutions to our problems and our hurts look more attractive than God's, people run. But we can't outrun God no matter how hard we try. He will always find us. He will always win.

Not long after my husband left, I recall standing at my kitchen counter completely void of any emotion other than despair. I was crying out to God, begging Him, pleading for Him to convict my husband's heart and cause him to come home. After thirty years, I simply didn't know how I was going to be able to pull it together. My hope of not only smiling again but living was depleted.

I have always written—journals, poems, attempts at novels, endless drafts of non-fiction work. I was the kid that loved it when my teacher would assign book reports. Writing papers in school came easy for me. I guess I was kind of a nerd that way.

Just before meeting my husband, I had self-published four children's books that were to be part of a preschool curriculum for a start-up enterprise that never quite got off the ground. (My attic still holds the remnants of that rather costly endeavor.) I had showed these books to my newly met, future husband. He was so very encouraging of my efforts, except that the illustrator I had hired for them was more of an amateur than I cared to admit. (Considering what I paid him, I can't complain.) I recall the conversation so well, how enthusiastically he told me that despite the pictures, the prose was "amazing." I had put my heart and soul into writing them. He was among the very first to tell me that he thought I had "a gift."

I fell in love with him right then and there. No lie.

With marriage came kids, and all the life that swirls and bends around raising them. Much of that life was wonderful. Most of it was. It was full, with all the blips and bleeps of normal ups and downs. It was just the ending that got messy. It was just the breaking part that changed our happily ever after.

I hated that part.

Accelerate the story many years to that fall afternoon, standing in my kitchen. I didn't want to accept that there was no hope for us. God, from whom I know all blessings come, couldn't leave me hanging like that. As much as I trusted Him, I wasn't sure He understood just how desperate I was for Him to fix my marriage, to mend the rift, and talk sense to the only man I had ever loved.

I needed a miracle. I needed God to part the Red Sea. I needed to look out my front window and see my husband's car pull up in the driveway, white flag flapping in the wind, and him running in to tell me he had made a big mistake.

I guess you already know how that worked out.

God, however, did give me a miracle of sorts. Granted, I didn't think of it as one at the time. Holding on to my counter, my shoulders heaving, gasping for breath from my fitful crying, I heard it.

"Write—your healing is there."

It wasn't a voice, but it was. It was unmistakably *not* mine. It ran across my consciousness like a laser, all my faculties mesmerized, imprinting it like a banner headline in my mind.

I stopped crying. Something shifted. What followed was the title, *When He Walks Away*. That was all I had to go on. I felt a little bit like what I imagine Moses must have thought when he saw the burning bush. "You want me to do what, God?"

Nevertheless, there was no denying it. I had a mandate. I could not ignore it. I could not pretend that I hadn't heard it. He knew that I did.

So I began. The title as my header, the thoughts came jumbling out of me. It was cathartic. Some chapters were much harder to write than others. I prayed, asking that they be His words, not mine. A lot of it, I wept as I wrote. Astoundingly, my thoughts were transformed like a block of ice chiseled into a beautifully sculptured swan. I only wanted to do what I promised Him I would, believing that He would do with it what He willed.

If there is one theme, one message that I hope I conveyed in these pages, I pray that it is the one that comes summed up in Romans 8:28:

> *And we know that in all things, God works*
> *for the good of those who love him, who have been*
> *called according to his purpose.*

There *is* a purpose to all of this, even when we can't see it yet.

This journey was not one I wanted to make. I'm sure, beyond all doubt, that the same can be said for you. But something echoes in the canyons when we are walking in the valley. It comes back to us like a boomerang. *We* come back to us. God comes to show us that He never left us, and He has a plan. Life comes full circle.

We know that we can never say never.

Things have happened that I would have not been able to predict. Just being on my own, the ending of a marriage I thought would last forever, the stories and blanks I wish I had never heard or watched be filled in.

Losing the man I loved and witnessing a transformation that is still hard to believe leaves their mark.

But God.

All the years that I never completed projects I had started, books and manuscripts stored away when life gave me every excuse to put them aside, lingered. They called me names like Procrastinator, Failure, and Insufficient.

I knew that this one had to have a different ending. I promised God.

I find it poetic, really. One of the last things my husband said to me right before he left, as I shared in my brokenness about how much I loved him, how much I adored him. I wanted only to make sure that he knew my heart could not sing without him. "All you've ever had are pretty words. They mean nothing."

If *his* words were daggers, I believe my heart would have been cut right out of my chest. Although it is not biblical, what goes around truly does come around again.

Here I am. Though this is not a self-published children's book, it is the first thing I have finished since the day I met the man who had once encouraged me so greatly on a September afternoon on Cape Cod so many years ago.

There are now bookends, each holding up the life we lived in between. The pictures are not great, but hopefully, the prose is good. I put my heart and soul into it.

My grandmother used to have a way of taking complex things and boiling them all down so that it was easy to see what was truly important. I would come to her, sharing my problems, my worries, the different scenarios of how I should deal with a particular issue. I would tell her what I hoped would happen as well as what I feared might.

Her response was always the same. "You never can tell," she would say. "Why don't you just let it all play out and see?" She knew how God worked.

How many, many times throughout my life, when burdens would weigh me down and fear would keep me up at night, would I think of Gram. Her sensibilities were keen and strong, and her faith even more so. She was my hero.

She was always right. We can't know what tomorrow brings, but God does.

We can't understand the reason for the trials we must endure, but God does.

We wander in the desert, weary in our unbelief, not sure when we will stumble into the season of our better days, but God does.

I told someone recently, "I have always trusted God, I have always had faith. Now I have a much greater, a much deeper knowing that He is with me. I know He is going to work everything out. It's all going to be okay."

I don't know *how* it will come about, but He does.

Because of what I have come through, I trust God more than I have ever trusted Him in all my life.

I want you to know, my fellow traveler, how very much I appreciate you letting me pour out to you what I feel that God has poured into me and through these words. It is an honor and a privilege to have been on this journey with you. I pray that in some small way, what is written here has helped.

Please know that you are not alone.

Don't stop believing for what your heart is yearning for. God hears your prayers. He knows everything you have been through and how He is going to turn it around for your good. It's a process to get to the place where you find the purpose in it.

Trust Him. You will smile again.

Just let it all play out and see.

It's hard to not feel
Alone
Dejected
Defeated
And inadequate
When all you ever believed in
Loved
Honored
And needed
Walks away
But it's not about you, it's about him—
his issues
his defeats
his inadequacies
his aloneness
And it's about Him—
Who yearns for you to Believe
that Better Days are ahead
Healing comes after the pain subsides
and sleep returns
And new dreams beckon your broken heart
to mend
"Have Faith," He says, "in Me."
I will lead you to another land
Where crops are plentiful
and love is True
And where dancing and joy return
In Full.
Believe it—
The Best Is Yet to Come.

From the author's journal

MARY A. BRYANT IS a passionate believer in God's healing and divine power at work in all who place their faith in Him. She has great empathy for issues of the heart and for those whose life circumstances have caused hurt and struggle. It is from this ground that she has witnessed the planting of God's greatest blessings, and she aspires to encourage the truth that He turns all things together for our good. As a speaker, she shares her life experience with grace, humor, and the inspirational message that in every storm, there is an anchor when one turns to their faith in God.

Mary lives in Charlotte, North Carolina, near her four young adult children. Although *When He Walks Away* is her first book, she has other works that will soon be published. For more information, please visit her website (www.marybryantbooks.com.)